DANGEROUS INSECTS

The Encyclopedia of Danger

DANGEROUS ENVIRONMENTS

DANGEROUS FLORA

DANGEROUS INSECTS

DANGEROUS MAMMALS

DANGEROUS NATURAL PHENOMENA

DANGEROUS PLANTS AND MUSHROOMS

DANGEROUS PROFESSIONS

DANGEROUS REPTILIAN CREATURES

DANGEROUS SPORTS

DANGEROUS WATER CREATURES

CHELSEA HOUSE PUBLISHERS

The Encyclopedia of Danger

DANGEROUS INSECTS

Missy Allen
Michel Peissel

CHELSEA HOUSE PUBLISHERS
New York   Philadelphia

THE ENCYCLOPEDIA OF DANGER includes general information on treatment and prevention of injuries and illnesses. The publisher advises the reader to seek the advice of medical professionals and not to use these volumes as first aid manual.

On the cover   Watercolor painting of a Human Botfly by Michel Peissel

Chelsea House Publishers

Editor-in-Chief   Remmel Nunn
Managing Editor   Karyn Gullen Browne
Picture Editor   Adrian G. Allen
Art Director   Maria Epes
Assistant Art Director   Howard Brotman
Manufacturing Director   Gerald Levine
Systems Manager   Lindsey Ottman

Encyclopedia of Danger
Editor   Karyn Gullen Browne

Staff for DANGEROUS INSECTS
Associate Editor   Terrance Dolan
Copy Editor   Ian Wilker
Production Editor   Marie Claire Cebrián
Designer   Diana Blume
Editorial Assistant   Karen Hirsch

Printed in Mexico.

First Printing

1 3 5 7 9 8 6 4 2

Library of Congress Cataloging–in–Publication Data

Peissel, Michel.
Dangerous insects/Michel Peissel, Missy Allen.
p. cm.—(The Encyclopedia of danger)
Summary: Examines twenty–five dangerous insects from around the world.
0–7910–1785–0   0–7910–1933–0 (pbk.)
1. Insects—Juvenile literature. 2. Insect pests—Juvenile literature. 3. Arthropoda, Poisonous—Juvenile literature. [1. Insects. 2. Insects pests. 3. Arhtropods, Poisonous. 4. Poisonous animals. 5. Dangerous animals.] I. Allen, Missy. II. Title. III. Series: Peissel, Michel, Encyclopedia of danger.
                                                                        91–42651
QL467.2.P45 1992   CIP
595.7'065—dc20   AC

CONTENTS

THE ENCYCLOPEDIA OF DANGER

"Mother Nature" is not always motherly; often, she behaves more like a wicked aunt than a nurturing parent. She can be unpredictable and mischievous—she can also be downright dangerous.

The word *danger* comes from the Latin *dominium*—"the right of ownership"—and Mother Nature guards her domain jealously indeed, using an ingenious array of weapons to punish trespassers. These weapons have been honed to a fatal perfection during millions of years of evolution, and they can be insidious or overwhelming, subtle or brutal. There are insects that spray toxic chemicals and insects that go on the march in armies a million strong; there are snakes that spit venom and snakes that smother the life from their victims; there are fish that inflict electric shocks and fish that can strip a victim to the bones; there are even trees that exude poisonous gases and flowers that give off a sweet—and murderous—perfume.

Many citizens of the modern, urban, or suburban world have lost touch with Mother Nature. This loss of contact is dangerous in itself; to ignore her is to invite her wrath. Every year, hundreds of children unknowingly provoke her anger by eating poisonous berries or sucking deadly leaves or roots; others foolishly cuddle toxic toads or step on venomous sea creatures. Naive travelers expose themselves to a host of unsuspected natural dangers, but you do not have to fly to a faraway country to encounter one of Mother Nature's sentinels; many of them can be found in your own apartment or backyard.

The various dangers featured in these pages range from the domestic to the exotic. They can be found throughout the world, from the deserts to the polar regions, from lakes and rivers to the depths of the oceans, from subterranean passages to high mountaintops, from rain forests to backyards, from barns to bathrooms. Which of these dangers is the most dangerous? We have prepared a short list of 10 of the most formidable weapons in Mother Nature's arsenal:

Grizzly bear.   Undoubtedly one of the most ferocious creatures on the planet, the grizzly needs little provocation to attack, maul, and maybe even eat a person. (There is something intrinsically more terrifying about an animal that will not only kill you but eat you—and not necessarily in that order—as well.) Incredibly strong, a grizzly can behead a moose with one swipe of its paw. Imagine what it could do to *you*.

Cape buffalo.   Considered by many big-game hunters to be the most evil-tempered animal in all of Africa, Cape buffalo bulls have been known to toss a gored body—perhaps the body of an unsuccessful big-game hunter—around from one pair of horns to another.

Weever fish.   The weever fish can inflict a sting so agonizing that victims stung on the finger have been known to cut off the finger in a desperate attempt to relieve the pain.

Estuarine crocodile.   This vile human-eater kills and devours an estimated 2,000 people annually.

Great white shark.   The infamous great white is a true sea monster. Survivors of great white shark attacks—and survivors are rare—usually face major surgery, for the great white's massive jaws inflict catastrophic wounds.

Army ants.   Called the "Genghis Khans of the insect world" by one entomologist, army ants can pick an elephant clean in a few days and routinely cause the evacuation of entire villages in Africa and South America.

Blue-ringed octopus.   This tentacled sea creature is often guilty of overkill; it frequently injects into the wound of a single human victim enough venom to kill 10 people.

Introduction

Black widow spider. The female black widow, prowler of crawl spaces and outhouses, produces a venom that is 15 times as potent as rattlesnake poison.

Lorchel mushroom. Never make a soup from these mushrooms—simply inhaling the fumes would kill you.

Scorpion. Beware the sting of this nasty little arachnid, for in Mexico it kills 10 people for every 1 killed by poisonous snakes.

DANGEROUS INSECTS

They are everywhere—the fantastic little creatures commonly known as *insects*. We humans flatter ourselves when we refer to our species, *Homo sapiens*, as the dominant life-form on this planet. In reality, it is the insects and their various cousins who are the most successful animals on earth. Sheer weight of numbers alone gives them the right to call the earth theirs; insects account for more than three–quarters of the world's life-forms. Close to a million different species have been identified, but entomologists (scientists who study insects) believe that there are probably several million more that have yet to be discovered. Add to this their remarkable adaptability and reproductive capabilities, and one begins to understand why most entomologists firmly believe that long after *Homo sapiens* has vacated the premises, ants, spiders, flies, and beetles will continue to thrive.

Because of their vast numbers and the great biological diversity of the insects and their cousins, entomologists have developed an international system of classification that is linked to the overall system used for identifying life on earth. The animal kingdom is divided into major categories called phyla. The creatures commonly referred to as insects belong to the phylum Arthropoda.

Arthropoda is made up of various subphyla, including Mandibulata and Chelicerata, which in turn are divided into classes. All the organisms featured in *Dangerous Insects* belong to two classes—Insecta and Arachnida. Insecta is part of the subphylum Mandibulata; Arachnida belongs to the subphylum Chelicerata. Each class is further broken down into various orders, then into suborders, which in turn are divided into superfamilies and then into families and subfamilies. Families and subfamilies are divided into genera, which are finally divided into species, the most exact grouping. In *Dangerous Insects*, we will be dealing mostly with various genera and species of the Insecta and Arachnida classes.

Class: Insecta

Insects are any of the many species of small invertebrate animals characterized primarily (but not always) by three pairs of jointed legs, two pairs of wings, an external skeleton (exoskeleton), a segmented body consisting of a head—which is equipped with sucking, piercing, or biting mouth parts (mandibles), two antennae, and compound eyes—a thorax, and an abdomen. As a group, insects feed upon just about every living thing on earth, and they thrive in almost every possible environment. All insects hatch from eggs, although with some species the eggs hatch within the abdomen of the female. Many insects undergo metamorphosis—a series of drastic changes in bodily form—as they grow to adulthood. In gradual, or incomplete metamorphosis, there are three stages: egg, larva, and adult. In complete metamorphosis, there are four stages: egg, larva, pupa, and adult.

Class: Arachnida

The arachnids are a class of small animals related to but considered distinct from the insects. Spiders, scorpions, mites, and ticks are arachnids, although they are often grouped under the general heading "insects." Arachnids are among the oldest land animals on earth. Unlike true insects, the head and thorax of the arachnid are fused into a single part—the cephalothorax. Arachnids usually have four pairs of legs, a pair of pedipalpi, or grasping appendages, and a pair of chelicerae, or jaws. They have simple eyes and no antennae. Arachnids are almost all predatory or parasitic, feeding on insects or larger animals. Most arachnids are hatched from eggs.

Introduction

In the animal kingdom, survival is the name of the game. In order to survive, an animal must be able to do two things—eat, and keep from being eaten or otherwise destroyed. It is no accident that so many different species of insects and arachnids have survived so well for so long; they are very good at defending themselves and eating. It is in the pursuit of these two essential activities—defending and feeding—that insects and arachnids pose a physical danger to humans. As predators and parasites, many insects and arachnids actively prey on humans, using them for food and (ugh!) as living hosts for their young, thus spreading disease and infection. Other insects and arachnids attack humans as a matter of self–defense—although many a wasp sting or ant bite seems more like a preemptive strike than an act of defense—and the stings and bites of these combative creatures range from moderately painful to excruciating to fatal.

Despite the horrors you will encounter on the following pages, insects and arachnids should not be reviled or held in contempt; any entomologist will gladly assure you that the benefits humankind and Earth's ecosystem derive from the insects and arachnids easily outweigh the negative aspects. Nor should you go out of your way to torment, stomp, smash, mutilate, or otherwise exterminate the bees, bugs, spiders, and ants of the world, unless it is absolutely necessary. For if you go looking for them with these things in mind, chances are they will turn the tables on you. Remember: There are a lot more of them than there are of us.

KEY

HABITAT

FOREST

SEA

WOOD/TRASH

TOWNS

SHORE

GRASS/FIELDS

MOUNTAINS

SWAMP/MARSH

GARDEN

FRESH WATER

JUNGLE

BUILDING

DESERT

CITIES

KEY

HOW IT GETS PEOPLE

INGESTION

TOUCH

STING

BITE

SPIT

SPRAY

MAUL

CLIMATIC ZONE

TEMPERATE

TROPICAL

ARCTIC

MORTALITY

ONE

TWO

THREE

FOUR

13

ANOPHELES MOSQUITO

Genus: Anopheles

HOW IT GETS PEOPLE

CLIMATIC ZONE

HABITAT

HABITAT

RATING

"If I passed my hand across my face I brought it away covered with blood and with the crushed bodies of gorged mosquitos," wrote explorer Michael Spruce, describing an expedition up South America's Orinoco River. The itchy torment of the mosquito bites was bad enough, but there was worse to come for Spruce, who soon contracted malaria.

Malaria—the mere mention of the word conjures up the image of a feverish Humphrey Bogart sweating and swatting his way up a steamy jungle river in the movie *The African Queen*. The scourge of the tropics, malaria has afflicted such adventurers as Sir Richard Burton, John Hanning Speke, James Richardson, and the famed explorer of Africa, Dr. David Livingstone. The renowned Mungo Park lost 34 of his 44 men to this mosquito–borne disease during an expedition up Africa's Niger River. Even the conqueror Alexander the Great was not immune.

Many historians believe that malarial fever eventually killed the mighty Alexander—something that even the fiercest warriors of the Persian Empire had failed to accomplish.

But the mosquitoes that carry and transmit malaria do not restrict themselves to explorers and conquerors. Malaria is the most common disease in the world. An estimated 97 million people are stricken annually, and 2.1 billion people are at risk. In Africa, the disease kills a million children every year. On the central highlands of Madagascar, an estimated 100,000 victims of malaria died in 1988, and in 1990 about 70% of the population of Tanzania was afflicted.

Name/Description

Anopheles is a genus of mosquito belonging to the family Culicidae. The smaller male mosquito ingests mainly flower nectar, whereas his voracious mate feeds on blood, needing its protein for egg production. The female uses her proboscis (an elongated sucking organ), which extends from her oral region and consists of six needlelike parts, to pierce the

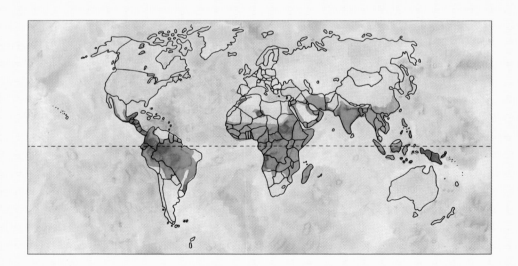

skin of her victim and extract blood. As the mosquito sucks, she pumps saliva into the wound to prevent her victim's blood from coagulating.

Infection

Anopheles mosquitoes carry malaria and 80 other serious diseases. Malaria is caused by one of four single–celled, parasitical organisms called plasmodia, which are carried in the female mosquito's saliva. After entering the victim's bloodstream, the plasmodia go directly to the liver, where they grow and multiply. They then invade red blood cells, where they again multiply, later moving on to fresh red blood cells. Each time they move they can trigger a new bout of malarial symptoms.

Symptoms

Malaria occurs in two forms: Benign malaria is a chronic, draining illness, but it is usually not life–threatening. Malignant malaria causes an agonizing death if the infected blood corpuscles reach the brain. Symptoms of benign malaria usually appear in 5 to 10 days, although there may be an incubation period of up to one year. Symptoms of benign malaria include fever, malaise, headache, abdominal pain, and jaundice.

Symptoms of malignant malaria evolve through three stages: a cold stage (hard, shaking chills and a rise in body temperature); a hot stage (body temperature climbs as high as 105 degrees Fahrenheit); and a sweating stage (body temperature falls, and profuse sweating begins). Victims may experience liver and kidney failure, severe anemia, delirium, convulsions, coma, and death.

Treatment

Although malaria was well on its way to eradication in the 1960s, it has once again become a major threat because in some parts of the world, *anopheles* mosquitoes have grown immune to insecticides, and

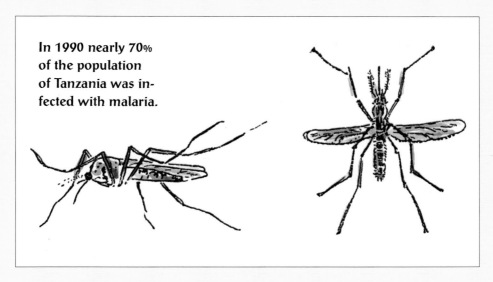

In 1990 nearly 70% of the population of Tanzania was infected with malaria.

the malarial parasites have developed an immunity to many of the antimalarial drugs on the market. Antimalarial drugs do not in fact prevent infection; rather, they inhibit the proliferation of the parasites in the liver. These drugs are usually only effective when medication begins two weeks before the user enters a malarial area (such as a jungle) and continues for up to six weeks after departure.

Prevention

• Mosquitoes attack at night. Cover up exposed skin between dusk and dawn, but avoid wearing dark clothing, after–shave lotion, and perfume, all of which attract mosquitoes.

• Sleep under mosquito netting with at least 26 holes per square inch.

• Apply mosquito repellents every two or three hours. There are now rather attractive wrist and ankle bands available that have been soaked in mosquito repellent and that are said to be quite effective.

• Take antimalarial drugs such as chloroquine, primaquine, or Fansidar.

ARMY ANT

CLIMATIC ZONE

Genera: Eciton and Anomma

RATING

HOW IT GETS PEOPLE

HOW IT GETS PEOPLE

HABITAT

HABITAT

They advance in massive, unbroken columns of as many as one and a half million ants, traveling at speeds of up to 20 miles per hour, pouring like a black tide over everything in their path. One such army is said to have taken 16 days and nights to pass. At the head of the columns, the ants separate into raiding parties to seek out prey; later, they close ranks again, forming a streamlined, two-inch-wide column. They are highly organized, moving and behaving as if they were a single organism. Albert Schweitzer, the famous missionary and physician, witnessed an invasion of army ants near his hospital in Gabon, West Africa, and was astonished by their military precision. (Schweitzer and his wife drove the invaders away with pails of water mixed with a strong disinfectant.)

Encountering prey, army ants in huge numbers quickly swarm over their victim, tearing away flesh with their sharp mandibles (biting jaws). They are vicious and tenacious. "A half-dozen [army ants] swarmed over me," recalled one victim, "drawing little gouts of blood with every bite and apparently burning the skin with a strong acid. Several had forced their jaws into the heavy leather of my boots. They hung on so venomously that they left their still active teeth in the leather after the rest of their bodies had been torn away." And the pain of their bite, recalled another man who had been unfortunate enough to experience it, "is impossible to conceive."

These tiny, voracious predators eat any animal they encounter; army ants have been known to devour wounded elephants, picking them clean in three days. Any creature not quick enough to get out of their way—including a human being—is fair game for the marauding army ants. In 1922, a professor addressing the Royal Institute in London on the subject of army ants cited an authentic case of a human baby that had been eaten alive by the ants. The inhabitants of one West African village tell the story of a British resident who drank too much gin and passed out on the roadside. Two days later, his skeleton was found. His bones were picked clean but he still wore his evening clothes.

Although it seems unbelievable, native South Americans often welcome the approach of an army ant column. They happily abandon their

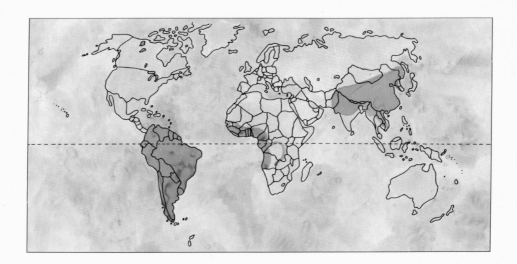

dwellings to the ants, knowing that by the time the fierce little soldiers are finished, all the unwelcome vermin, from rats to cockroaches to scorpions, will have been eaten or chased out. Once the ants are gone, the villagers can return to a newly cleaned home.

Name/Description

Army ants, of the genus *Eciton* in South America and *Anomma* in Africa (where they are also known as driver ants), are social, nomadic ants that move in vast armies. They are defined as social because their so-called army, which is actually a colony on the move, is divided into castes consisting of the short-lived, winged males; the queen; the female workers; and the female soldiers, which are actually large workers equipped with oversized, saberlike mandibles. They range from a quarter-inch to a half-inch long, and their primary food sources are other insects and their larvae.

Army ants are nomadic. Their wandering is cyclic and corresponds to the reproductive cycle of the army's single queen. When they are not on the move, they take up temporary quarters in hollow trees, empty burrows, or spaces between stones. Unable to stand the hot tropical sun (direct sunlight can kill them in two minutes), army ants usually march only after sundown, although they will sometimes move on cloudy days or through the shade in a forest. If the sun does strike a column, the soldiers will form themselves into a tube about an inch in diameter, through which the queen and the workers can travel. (This tube is so strong that it can be lifted up off the ground without breaking.) They might also build a tunnel of earth mixed with their saliva. They are extraordinarily strong, and they are impervious to water; an army ant can survive for up to six hours underwater.

Injury

Army ants attack with a curious jumping motion. Their huge, sharp mandibles can easily pierce human skin, leaving small, jagged wounds.

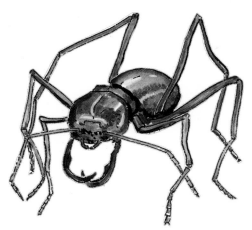

Army ants have been known to pick a wounded elephant clean in less than three days.

Because they attack in overwhelming numbers, a human victim might be quickly covered with such wounds.

Symptoms

An army ant bite may cause irritation of the skin, along with inflammation and blistering. Secondary infections may develop.

Treatment

Wash wounds immediately with soap and water. Depending on the extent of the injury, tetanus shots or a broad–spectrum antibiotic may be administered.

Prevention

• Stay out of their way.

BLACK WIDOW SPIDER

HOW IT GETS PEOPLE

Species: Lactrodectus mactans

RATING

HABITAT

HABITAT

HABITAT

HABITAT

HABITAT

HABITAT

CLIMATIC ZONE

CLIMATIC ZONE

Pity the male black widow spider, for his mate is a harsh mistress. After fertilization by a male of her species, the female black widow often eats him (thus making herself a "widow"). This notorious arachnid can be just as cruel to a human who intrudes on her sanctuary, although she is unpredictable. The black widow can inflict a nonpoisonous bite that is no more painful or dangerous than a pinprick. She can also use her hollow fangs to inject a potentially deadly venom into a victim—a venom that is 15 times more potent than the venom of a rattlesnake. One survivor of a black widow envenomization endured what he described as "huge tidal waves" of excruciating pain.

Name/Description

Lactrodectus mactans, known as the black widow, is a venomous New World spider. Black widows are also known as shoe–button spiders, red–mark spiders, red–back spiders, jockey spiders, and hourglass spiders. The female black widow is usually black, but it can also be yellow or white. It grows to about a half–inch in length and has an hourglass-shaped red mark on its abdomen. Inhabiting dry, dark places, the female spins a coarse, strong, irregular web to trap insects for food.

   Only the female black widow presents a danger to humans; the male is too small to produce enough venom to hurt a larger creature. The female poisons her victims by flexing the striated muscles that surround her venom glands, forcing the venom forward into her sharp, hollow fangs, which she uses to inject the poison into her prey. If her prey is

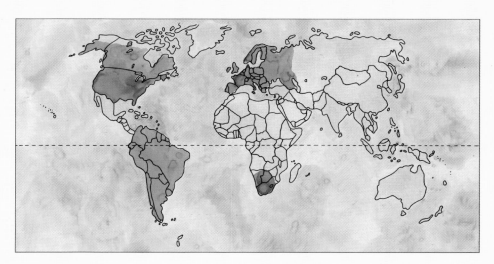

too small to pose a threat to her, the black widow may forgo poisoning and simply tear it apart. The spider digests its meal externally, vomiting digestive fluid onto it. When the meal has been broken down into a palatable soup by this fluid, the black widow feeds.

Toxicology

The black widow's venom is neurotoxic, affecting the central nervous system. Its exceptional potency has been recognized for centuries. The Gosiute Indians of Utah mixed the macerated bodies of black widows with rattlesnake venom to create a lethal poison for their arrowheads.

Symptoms

The bite may be relatively mild. Two tiny red dots accompanied by slight swelling may appear at the site of the bite. If poisoned, the victim's stomach muscles will become rigid. Abdominal pain will be followed by widespread cramps and pain lasting for 12 to 48 hours and accompanied by headache, dizziness, nausea and vomiting, rash, sweating, a rapid and feeble pulse, fever, urticaria (hives), increased blood pressure, convulsions, and possibly death. When death does occur, shock is a contributing factor.

Treatment

Keep the victim quiet and warm. Morphine or calcium gluconate may be administered for pain; sedatives, short-acting barbiturates, and Robaxin may be given for muscle spasms. A black widow antiserum is available in some countries, including the United States.

Prevention

• The introduction of modern plumbing has significantly reduced the incidence of black widow envenomizations; nearly half the black widow

Drop for drop, the black widow spider's venom is 15 times more poisonous than that of the prairie rattlesnake.

bites reported in medical literature during the first four decades of this century were inflicted by spiders lurking under outdoor lavatory seats.

• Avoid darkened corners of attics, barns, basements, abandoned build‐ings—and outhouses.

BLISTER BEETLE

HOW IT GETS PEOPLE

Species: Lytta vesicatoria

HABITAT

CLIMATIC ZONE

RATING

The blister beetle is both a blessing and a curse to farmers. In the larval stage, blister beetles are welcomed by farmers, because they eat grasshopper eggs, and grasshoppers are notoriously destructive to crops. As adults, however, blister beetles develop a ravenous appetite for many of the same crops they once helped to protect from the grasshoppers.

The blister beetle has been both a blessing and a curse to healers and physicians as well. Blister beetles secrete a fluid known as cantharidin. For centuries, cantharidin has been used for various medicinal purposes. But cantharidin is a dangerous substance, as agricultural workers who come into contact with blister beetles can attest. And medicinal preparations made from cantharidin often do more harm than good. Internal cantharidin poisoning can be fatal. External cantharidin reactions usually occur as a result of direct contact with the beetle. A blister beetle can scuttle across a person's chest without causing any harm, but the slightest pressure on the beetle, such as an attempt to brush it away, will force it to secrete cantharidin, a clear, sticky fluid that will cause unsightly, irritating blisters to develop on the victim's skin. The severity of the blisters will depend on the amount of cantharidin excreted by the beetle. Thus, if a person panics and crushes the trespassing beetle against his or her skin, a lot of cantharidin will be released, and gargantuan blisters are likely to appear.

Those who collect blister beetles for use in medicines are understandably cautious. First, they cover themselves from head to toe. Then, early in the morning when it is still chilly, they spread muslin cloths beneath trees inhabited by the beetles. Gatherers then climb up the trees and shake down the startled beetles, which are too numb and sluggish from the cold to escape. The bundle of beetles is then plunged into hot water mixed with vinegar, which kills the beetles. The dead insects are then dried in lofts or outside on paper sheets. When dried, they are packed—by workers still wearing gloves—in airtight boxes, or in glass or earthenware vessels, and are stored until needed for medicinal preparations.

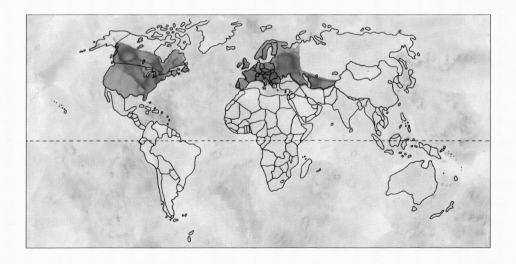

Name/Description

The blister beetle, *Lytta vesicatoria*, sometimes called the Spanish fly or the oil beetle, is a crinotoxic (excreting poison through pores), winged, bright green insect common to the United States, Canada, Europe, and southern Russia. The blister beetle has a slender, leathery body of up to an inch in length, and two functioning wings protected by wing covers of a metallic green or blue color. The wing covers are often marked with bands or stripes. Blister beetles have an unusual life cycle that involves a succession of different larval stages. Their long, powerful legs allow them to hop about with great agility. Blister beetles are said to smell like mice.

Toxicology/Pharmacology

Cantharidin, the substance secreted by blister beetles as a defense mechanism, is the oldest of all insect medicines. It has been used to treat a wide variety of ailments—including warts, dropsy, apoplexy, jaundice, pleurisy, pericarditis, sciatica, impotence, and, ironically, skin blisters—for more than 2,000 years. Cantharidin is a urinary tract irritant; it acquired its reputation as an aphrodisiac because ingestion can lead to priapism (an abnormal, more or less persistent, and often painful erection of the penis).

Symptoms

External exposure to cantharidin will cause no immediate discomfort, although a tingling sensation may be noticed about 10 minutes after contact. Blisters will develop at the contact site in 8 to 12 hours. If the beetle was actually crushed or pressed against the skin, there will be greater irritation and very large blisters.

Internal cantharidin poisoning is usually the result of an accidental overdose, which can cause intense pain in the alimentary canal, in the stomach and kidneys, and in the urinary tract. There may be vomiting, priapism, diarrhea (sometimes bloody), and a persistent desire to urin–

It takes only two one-thousandths of an ounce of blister beetle poison to kill an adult human.

ate, accompanied by a weak pulse and followed, in severe cases, by profound collapse and death.

Treatment

Blisters from external exposure should disappear within a few hours. If they are very irritating, a soothing lotion, such as calamine, may be applied. For ingestion of cantharidin, induce vomiting immediately by giving an emetic, or have the stomach pumped.

Prevention

- Blister beetles are night fliers. After dark, be alert around sources of bright light, which attract the beetles, and near areas where common agricultural crops are present.
- If a blister beetle lands on you, brush it away as gently as possible.
- Even a tiny amount of cantharidin is extremely dangerous; it should be used only under the strict supervision of a qualified physician.

BUFFALO GNAT

HOW IT GETS PEOPLE

Family: Simuliidae

HABITAT

CLIMATIC ZONE

CLIMATIC ZONE

RATING

Like something out of a horror movie, buffalo gnats travel in cloudlike swarms that darken the sky. Persistent little devils, they have been known to follow victims for miles. They are especially fond of eyes, ears, and noses, but they will bite any exposed skin. Although there is no documented record of a human fatality, the animal carnage has been astounding. In a single year, buffalo gnats in Romania killed 17,474 horses and other livestock. A decade later, in Yugoslavia, over 11,000 head of cattle were killed. Many of these animals were *smothered* to death by dense clouds of buffalo gnats.

Avoiding the buffalo gnat is difficult for people as well as for animals. Biting insects are attracted to humans for many reasons—their body odor, perfume, the color of their clothing, or the food they are eating or drinking. Buffalo gnats are drawn to the carbon dioxide exhaled by humans; they are also attracted by a person's body heat. People can mask their body odor, refrain from eating and drinking outdoors, and refrain from wearing certain clothing or perfume. But they cannot voluntarily lower their body temperature or stop breathing. In an area where the buffalo gnat is common, it is almost inevitable that humans will be bitten.

Name/Description

The buffalo gnat, also known as the blackfly, is a tiny, humpbacked, bloodsucking member of the Simuliidae family of flies. Found in most parts of the world and especially in northern regions, the buffalo gnat has two broad, iridescent wings and two sharp piercing/sucking proboscises, which the female uses to suck the blood she needs for ovarian development. (The males feed on nectar.) In spite of being called black, these flies are often colored in shades ranging from charcoal to light gray to yellow.

Buffalo gnat larvae are found in swiftly flowing, preferably cold waters, where they breed by the millions. Females lay egg clusters on

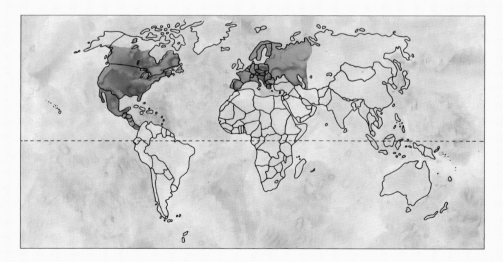

sticks, rocks, or plants below the surface. The eggs hatch in several days, producing multitudes of aquatic larvae—2,880 larvae were reportedly taken from a stone 10 inches in diameter. The larvae use suction plates or the spider–web–like threads they spin to cling to plants and rocks. Sometimes they will travel along the threads in the fashion of an inchworm.

After several weeks, the larvae will enter the intermediate, or pupal, stage of development. As pupae, they live in a basket–shaped, aquatic cocoon, from which they project two bundles of long, thin, silvery threads that extract oxygen from the water. In a week or two, fully developed buffalo gnats will emerge, float to the surface, and fly away to begin their bloodsucking careers. There can be up to six generations born per year.

Toxicology

People who have been attacked by buffalo gnats initially feel no pain, because the gnat injects an anesthetic substance into the skin around the wound. But she also injects a neurotoxin that irritates the skin and that may have a pronounced effect on the glands around the ears and neck.

Symptoms

Because of the anesthetic carried in the buffalo gnat's saliva, the only immediate sign of an attack—aside from the presence of the gnats themselves—may be a tiny drop of blood near the wound. The anesthetic usually wears off within an hour, and then a painful, itchy wheal forms on the skin. After a few days, these irritating welts may develop blisterlike lumps or hard pus–filled lumps that may last for up to a month.

Occasionally, the victim may display symptoms similar to the symptoms of mastoiditis (inflammation of the mastoid—the bones of the inner ear—and mastoid cells.) Multiple bites can produce a high fever

Buffalo gnats can travel in swarms so dense that they blacken the sky in midday.

and in some cases anaphylactic shock, a severe allergic reaction that can result in death. (For symptoms of anaphylactic shock, see Hymenoptera Stings, p. 114.)

Treatment

Wash the bitten area well with soap and water. If the skin is broken, apply an antiseptic. Apply an anesthetic cream containing benzocaine to control the itching; oral antihistamines may also help. (For prevention and treatment of anaphylactic shock, see Hymenoptera Stings, p. 114.)

Prevention

- Cover up with long–sleeved shirts, long trousers, socks, etc.
- Space spray or fogger insect repellents may provide temporary protection outside.
- Apply an insect repellent to skin or clothing.
- Avoid white light bulbs, which attract buffalo gnats.

BULLDOG ANT

HOW IT GETS PEOPLE

Species: Myrmecia gulosa

HOW IT GETS PEOPLE

HABITAT

HABITAT

HABITAT

HABITAT

CLIMATIC ZONE

CLIMATIC ZONE

RATING

The bulldog ant of Australia is aptly named—it is perhaps the most ferocious of the 10,000 species of ants found worldwide. Not only does it inflict painful bites with its massive, serrated mandibles, it can also inject venom into an unwary Aussie through a retractable stinger. Although it usually takes about 30 stings to kill a human, one unfortunate Australian horticulturalist was stung only once in her garden and died within a quarter of an hour.

Bulldog Ant

Compared to most of their sophisticated ant cousins, bulldog ants are evolutionary primitives. Their colonies, or nests, are unusually small, often housing only 500 members—a tiny village compared to the great, moving metropolises of higher ant orders such as army ants. The bulldog ants are socially backward as well; they do not have the organizational capabilities that allow other ant communities to function as a single, self-perpetuating organism. For example, each bulldog ant hunts and forages alone, and they cannot engage in trophallaxis, a method of communal feeding practiced by the higher ants—as well as termites, social bees, and wasps—in which regurgitated food is passed from mouth to mouth. (Actually, living in small groups and not passing regurgitated food around seems rather sophisticated.)

The queen of the bulldog ant colony has absolute power. Her tremendous egg output produces female workers and winged daughter queens. Once a year, the reigning queen will also produce a few winged males, who will mate with the young queens in a once-in-a-lifetime nuptial flight. During this aerial honeymoon, a young queen will accumulate enough spermatozoa to last her entire life—about a decade.

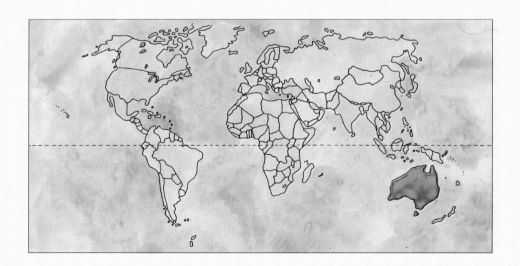

(The males, exhausted, die soon after.) The new queens then discard their wings and go underground to found colonies of their own. The heavily armed workers defend these colonies aggressively from any distur-bances, rushing out to attack if even a shadow falls across their nest. It is these vigilant workers who pose a threat to humans.

Name/Description

The bulldog ant, *Myrmecia gulosa*, is a primitive hunting ant. Bulldog ants are found only in Australia and Tasmania. They are quite large—up to an inch in length—and bright reddish brown in color. Their legs are extremely powerful, allowing them to run with great speed and to leap for distances of seven or eight inches—an extraordinary feat for a creature the size of a bulldog ant. They also have the alarming ability to leap backward by using their large mandibles as springs. Adult bulldog ants survive primarily on nectar; they hunt and kill other insects as a food source for their larvae. Like any good parent, the adult bulldog ant cuts this food into little pieces before feeding it to her young.

Injury/Toxicology

The powerful mandibles of the bulldog ant can leave a jagged, painful wound. The stinger injects what is thought to be a neurotoxin into the victim.

Symptoms

A bulldog ant bite causes moderate pain, but according to one victim, a sting feels like "a hot needle" going into one's flesh. Pain from a bulldog ant sting can last for up to 10 days.

Treatment

The area of a bite or sting should be thoroughly washed with an antiseptic, and if one is available, a corticosteroid lotion should be applied. An analgesic may be given for pain.

An Australian woman died just 15 minutes after receiving a single sting from a bulldog ant.

Prevention

- When in nonurban locations of Australia or Tasmania, do not go barefoot outside, and be on the alert for bulldog ant nests, which are conspicuously marked by mounds of excavated earth.

COCKROACH

HOW IT GETS PEOPLE

Family: Blattidae

HOW IT GETS PEOPLE

HABITAT

HABITAT

CLIMATIC ZONE

CLIMATIC ZONE

CLIMATIC ZONE

RATING

Today's cockroach is hardly distinguishable from its distant ancestors, some of which thrived as far back as 280 million years ago, during the prehistoric Carboniferous period. The ubiquitous cockroach has been on Earth 360 times longer than humankind, and many paranoid cockroach-haters are certain that those millions of years were spent concocting nefarious schemes to drive *Homo sapiens* mad. Legion from New York to Botswana, cockroaches are the ultimate survivors of the insect world, as their age—and their numbers—attest. In a sewer in Minneapolis, Minnesota, 3,000 cockroaches were discovered crowded into only 12 square feet; 2,500 were captured in a single night in an African hut; and around 75,000 were found in a four-room apartment in Austin, Texas.

Cockroaches are almost universally despised as vermin, and indeed, they are foul-smelling, filthy little creatures who leave a disgusting trail of spittle and excrement wherever they go. In spite of their squalidness, however, cockroaches are greatly prized by entomologists and other scientists, partly because they "require no more than a warm and cozy cage, a little water, and an occasional dog biscuit" to survive, as one researcher put it, and partly because of their remarkable physiological attributes. For example, cockroaches, which have been used in research on cancer, animal behavior, and nutrition, among other things, are among the few insects that can be taught to run through a maze. They can even be trained after their head has been removed! It took entomologist G. A. Horridge of Saint Andrew's University in Scotland only 30 minutes to teach a decapitated cockroach to keep its legs raised in order to avoid painful electric shocks. A headless cockroach can survive for a week before it starves to death.

Adaptability is the operative word when the cockroach is discussed. Consider the "TV cockroach." Originally inhabiting East Africa, this species is now found all over the world, for it has adapted to life in the back of television sets, where it feeds contentedly on glue, insulation,

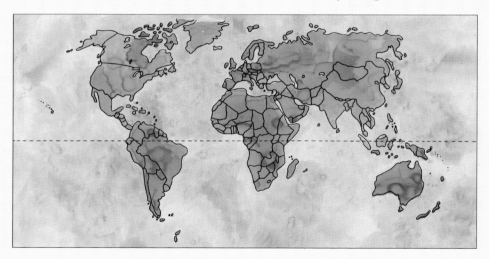

and other television components. Cockroaches will also eat wool, soap, paint, leather (especially shoes and old book bindings), cigar butts, and coffee grinds. One of their favorite snacks is the glue found on the back of postage stamps and wallpaper. They are also fond of human hair and fingernails. Cockroaches in Brazil have been known to nibble the eyelashes of sleeping infants, and sailors aboard roach–infested vessels sometimes sleep with gloves on to protect their fingernails.

Cockroaches like dark crevices, nooks, and tunnels—including the human ear. Many emergency rooms have reported cases of ear infestation. "It feels like something moving and scratching around in there," is the usual complaint. A doctor in New Orleans, who removed a cockroach from *both* of a patient's ears, said that they were "regular–size roaches, the kind you might see scurrying around the kitchen. . . . Ear canals are pretty sensitive and the bugs can cause painful sensations as they buzz and flip their wings."

Name/Description

The 3,500 species of cockroach belonging to the Blattidae family have a flat, oval body, and range from dirty tan to brownish black in color. They are winged insects, although many species are flightless. The head cannot be seen from above because it is concealed by the *pronotum*, or neck. Their antennae are long and slender, and they have multisegmented tails that are covered with tiny, remarkably sensitive hairs. The largest of the cockroaches measures about two and a half inches in length, with a seven–and–a–half–inch wingspan. Females lay their eggs in a beanlike capsule that protrudes visibly from their abdomen. The cockroach has a lifespan of five months to a year.

Toxicology/Injury

Not only are they ugly and smelly, cockroaches track around a good deal of human filth and carry a number of diseases, including polio, typhoid, gastroenteritis, and hepatitis. They also leave inky trails of bacteria–ridden spittle and excrement, and thus their presence in a human ear can cause secondary infections as well as considerable discomfort.

The resilient cockroach can survive an entire week after being decapitated; even then, they die only of starvation.

Symptoms
"It feels like something moving and scratching around in there. . . ."

Treatment
Unless you somehow manage to get the cockroach to leave your ear voluntarily, go to a doctor. Physicians through the years have dealt with this situation in a number of ways. They have been known to kill the trespassing cockroach by squirting mineral oil or a similar substance into the ear until the bug suffocated, after which it could be removed with tweezers. One doctor zapped the cockroach with the anesthetic lidocaine. The cockroach, reported the doctor, then "exited the ear canal at a convulsive rate of speed."

Pharmacology
Jamaican Indians use a mixture containing cockroach ashes to eliminate worms in children. In Russia, a cockroach powder called *Tarakane* was a popular treatment for dropsy.

In Peru, influenza is still treated with doses of cockroach powder.

Prevention
- Make sure that all pipelines in your house, building, or apartment are tightly sealed.
- Seal any cracks in the walls.
- Clean up dining areas immediately after you eat.
- For infested areas, use any of the anticockroach systems currently available.

FIRE ANT

Genus: Solenopsis

HOW IT GETS PEOPLE

HOW IT GETS PEOPLE

HABITAT

HABITAT

HABITAT

CLIMATIC ZONE

CLIMATIC ZONE

RATING

"When their mound is disturbed, these ants attack by sinking powerful jaws into the skin, then repeatedly thrust their poisonous stingers into the flesh. Fire ants may attack and kill newborn pigs, calves, sheep, and other animals; newly hatched chicks; and the young of ground–nesting birds."

Thus does the U.S. Department of Agriculture describe one of its archenemies, the fire ant. This fierce little warrior was accidentally imported from South America into Alabama in 1919. Like army ants, fire ants usually attack en masse, swarming over the victim and inflicting as many as 3,000 to 5,000 stings in a few seconds. Worker fire ants possess both mandibles and a venomous abdominal stinger. During an attack, the fire ant will latch onto a victim with its jaws and then pivot, stinging repeatedly in a circular pattern. Fire ants that have lost their stinger have been known to spray venom from the tip of their abdomen into a wound made by the mandibles.

The fire ant's venom is quite toxic and causes a fiery burning sensation and unsightly blistering. Some victims—usually, but not always, those with an allergic history or an acquired sensitivity to fire ant venom—lapse into anaphylactic shock. A 37–year–old Canadian man on his first trip outside Canada had car trouble while in Florida and was stung about 15 times by fire ants as he lay working under his car on the side of the road. Anaphylactic symptoms developed rapidly, and by the time he arrived at a hospital emergency room in St. Petersburg, he was unconscious and turning blue. Luckily, he responded well to treatment and survived. After recovery, he cut his vacation short and returned to his native Canada, where there are no fire ants.

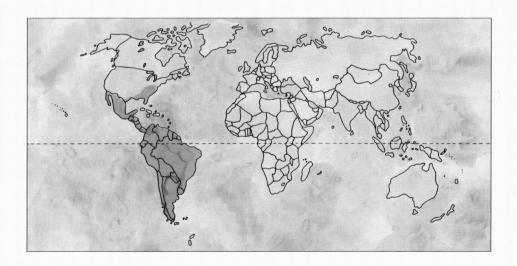

Dangerous Insects

Name/Description

Fire ants are any of the four species of the genus *Solenopsis*. They are brownish red in color, small—growing no larger than a quarter-inch in length—and omnivorous. Like other ants, they have a constricted waist, and their antennae are elbowed. Fire ant workers are sterile, wingless, and equipped with biting mandibles and a stinging apparatus. Fire ants build large nests of up to four feet in height (although three-quarters of the nest is underground) and three feet in diameter. A single acre can hold more than 100 of these earthen mounds, each of which houses between 50,000 and 250,000 ants.

Fire ants currently infest areas in several states in the southern United States, where they are decidedly unwelcome. In addition to the dangers posed by their aggressive nature, fire ants are perceived as a threat to commercial agriculture. According to the Department of Agriculture, "This ant damages vegetable crops by sucking juices from the stems of plants and by gnawing holes in roots, stalks, buds, ears, and pods. It injures pasture grasses, cereal and forage crops, nursery stock, and fruit trees." And the fire ants' elevated nests are said to have caused extensive damage to farm machinery. Conversely, the fire ant is considered to be a beneficial creature in its native South America because of the numerous troublesome insects it eats, including termites, weevils, beetles, aphids, snails, and spiders.

Toxicology

Fire ant venom is very potent and produces both immediate and delayed effects. The venom contains piperine alkaloids found nowhere else in the animal world.

Symptoms

At first, the sting of the fire ant causes severe, burning pain. Localized wheals form and develop into tiny blisters, which eventually become

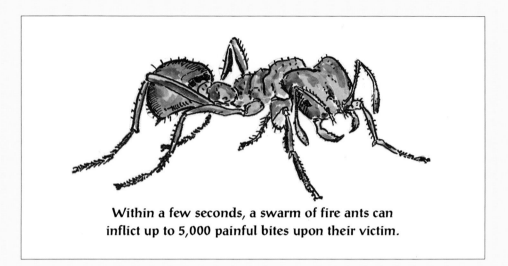

Within a few seconds, a swarm of fire ants can inflict up to 5,000 painful bites upon their victim.

filled with pus. After several days they will be replaced by scar tissue. (For symptoms of anaphylactic shock, see Hymenoptera Stings, p. 114.)

Treatment

For a nonallergic person who has only received a few fire ant stings, the wound should be carefully cleaned. Remove any remaining stinger parts and apply a paste of baking soda and water. (For treatment of anaphylactic shock, see Hymenoptera Stings, p. 114.)

Prevention

- If you have been previously bitten by fire ants and live in an area where they are common, you may want to undergo a course of hyposensitization injection therapy, which will consist of a few months of weekly injections of diluted fire-ant venom extract.
- If you are in an area known to be infested with fire ants, dress appropriately with shoes, long socks, and long trousers.

FUNNEL-WEB SPIDER

CLIMATIC ZONE

Genus: Atrax

RATING

HOW IT GETS PEOPLE

HOW IT GETS PEOPLE

HABITAT

HABITAT

Australia, haven for so many nasty little creatures, is the only place in the world where one might encounter the dreaded funnel-web spider. The most poisonous of Australia's 30 venomous arachnids, funnel-web spiders inject a powerful toxic agent that can kill a child within 15 minutes and an adult within 90.

The funnel-web spider is extremely ill-tempered. If approached—and it is hard to imagine anyone wanting to approach anything so repug-nant—the female will exude a clearly visible globule of poison from the tips of its fangs. Those who fail to heed this warning pay dearly. A seven-year-old Australian boy, sitting on his kitchen floor one morning, was bitten by a funnel-web spider. The boy was hospitalized, and although he seemed to be in good condition, he was kept overnight for observation. By the time his doctor arrived at the hospital the next morning, the youngster was near death. His pulse was weak, his breathing was shallow, his skin was pallid and cold to the touch, his lips were blue, and his temperature was so far below normal that it was unmeasurable.

This boy was lucky—he survived the attack and made a full recovery. But other victims of funnel-web spider envenomization have been less fortunate. An especially tragic case involved a pregnant woman who was attacked while hiking with her husband through the bush about 95 miles south of Sydney. Bitten by a funnel-web spider that had crawled inside her blouse, the woman collapsed. She was rushed to a nearby hospital, where efforts to save her and the unborn baby were in vain.

Name/Description

The funnel-web spider, of the genus *Atrax*, is a small, smooth, black mygalomorph (tarantula, or primitive spider), found only in Australia. From its long spinnerets (nipplelike organs with which spiders spin silk),

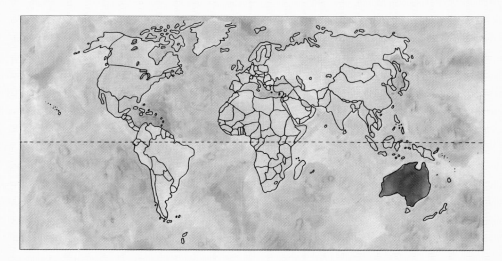

it weaves large, dense funnel webs that lead to the entrance of its lair. When an insect is trapped in the web, the spider comes out of its lair to attack and feed. Sometimes it preserves its meal by enshrouding it in silk webbing.

The male funnel–web spider may be unique among the arachnid brotherhood in that it is much more venomous than the female. Although the female may be half again as large as the male, growing up to an inch and a half in length whereas the male seldom surpasses an inch, and although she has larger poison glands and longer fangs, her venom is only about one–sixth as toxic as the male's.

In most spiders, the fangs open horizontally. In mygalomorphs, however, the fangs open and close vertically. Even if the threat of poison is disregarded, the fangs of the funnel–web spider are formidable weapons. According to one researcher, they can penetrate the skull of a chicken.

Toxicology

The funnel–web spider's poison glands are connected to the base of the fangs by a poison duct. The poison is injected into the victim with a downward stabbing action. The venom is powerfully neurotoxic and also contains digestive enzymes.

Symptoms

Immediately upon receiving a bite from a funnel–web spider, the victim will feel severe pain around the site of the puncture wound, followed by numbness in the same area. Nausea, vomiting, heavy sweating, and a general collapse will ensue. Respiration will become labored as the lungs become filled with fluid. Acute symptoms include cyanosis (bluish discoloration of the skin), frothing at the mouth, and cramps in the arms, legs, and abdomen. Untreated, these symptoms will lead to convulsions, coma, and death.

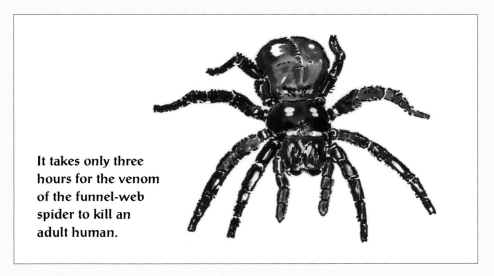

It takes only three hours for the venom of the funnel-web spider to kill an adult human.

Treatment

Although there is a specific and effective funnel–web spider antivenin in Australia, it is not always readily available for emergency use. Other antivenins have been successfully used to treat victims of the funnel–web spider. The little boy who was bitten in his kitchen was treated with tiger–snake antivenin. Certain drugs have proved effective as well. In December 1971, doctors in Sydney saved the life of a three year old who had been bitten. The little girl, who was found with the spider still clinging to her shoulder, was successfully treated with the drug athrophine.

Prevention

- When in Australia, be on guard for funnel–web spiders in gardens, yards, fields, beaches, sheds, houses, or wherever you go.
- When in Australia, always look inside your shoes or boots before you put them on.

HORNET

HOW IT GETS PEOPLE

Family: Vespidae

HOW IT GETS PEOPLE

HABITAT

HABITAT

HABITAT

HABITAT

HABITAT

CLIMATIC ZONE

RATING

"A hot, prickly sensation began at the back of my neck and crept forward, then up toward my face. A similar sensation, though milder, spread through my groin. My face felt flushed, my heart began to beat a crazy rhythm, and an intense and uncontrollable anxiety was rapidly taking hold of me.

"My lips started going numb. My tongue felt numb too—thick and heavy, as if shot with Novocain. My heartbeat was getting louder and more erratic, and there was a loud ringing in my ears. I felt slightly dizzy; my mouth was dry. I glanced at my face in the rearview mirror. The skin was shriveling up, puckering. And, most frightening of all, my windpipe was slowly closing off."

This harrowing description of an allergic reaction to multiple hornet stings was given by Richard Hall, a volunteer bus driver for senior citizens in Massachusetts. Fortunately for Hall, his bus was equipped with a CB radio. Had he not been able to radio ahead to a fire station so that the appropriate medical assistance was waiting for him, he might not have lived to tell about the episode.

Hornets have a bad reputation, and it is well deserved. A chemist who was asked what substances he would use to make a singularly torturous toxic agent replied that the chemical components of hornet venom would do the trick. And the hornet is feared all over the world. In November 1966, during the Vietnam War, Vietcong guerrillas reportedly placed a barricade of *hornet nests* on a highway to block an advancing column of South Vietnamese troops.

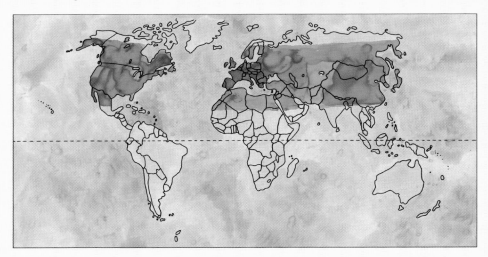

The terror that the hornet inspires sometimes helps to make their sting all the more deadly. The panic of a hornet-attack victim increases his or her circulation, causing the venom to spread throughout the body faster than it would if the victim remained calm and composed. Richard Hall, the Massachusetts bus driver, was apparently a cool customer indeed; had he panicked, he never would have made it to the fire station.

Name/Description

Hornets comprise the four genera—*Dolichovespula*, *Paravespula*, *Vespula*, and *Vespa*—of the Vespidae family of large, aggressive, social wasps. They are characterized by a winged, black, stout body with yellow or whitish markings. The face may be a solid yellow or white—thus the common names yellow-faced hornet and white-faced hornet. Hornets are more aggressive and inflict a more painful sting than other wasps or bees. Their stingers are generally larger and sharper than bee stingers, and because they lack barbs they allow the hornet to sting repeatedly. The largest of the hornets is appropriately called the giant hornet. Found in Europe and the northeastern United States, the giant hornet can grow to one and a third inches in length.

Hornets are social insects, nesting in groups. Their football-shaped nests are made of a coarse, gray, paperlike substance that the hornets produce by chewing wood to a pulp. Some hornets build nests attached to trees, bushes, or houses; others build subterranean nests. A single nest may contain thousands of hornets.

Toxicology

The principal toxic elements of hornet venom are serotonin, acetyl-choline, and histamines.

Symptoms

There is an old saying that it only takes three hornet stings to kill a man and seven to kill a horse. But it really takes 30 or more stings to kill an

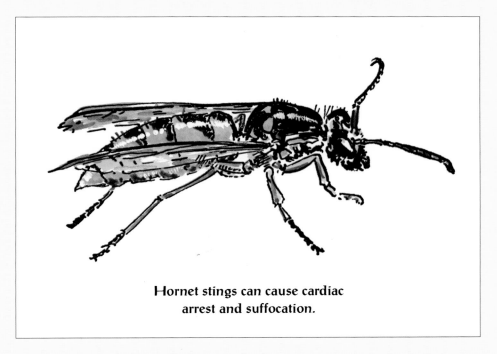

**Hornet stings can cause cardiac
arrest and suffocation.**

adult human. Nevertheless, a single hornet sting is quite painful and can
be dangerous if it is inflicted in the wrong place. A sting on the tongue,
for example, can result in such swelling that it becomes difficult for the
victim to breathe. And a sting on a large blood vessel can result in
internal bleeding.

Treatment

(For treatment of anaphylactic shock, see Hymenoptera Stings, p. 114.)

Prevention

• If you encounter a hornet nest, do not approach it. Keep children and
pets away. Do not attempt to remove the nest yourself—call an exterminator.

HUMAN BOTFLY

HOW IT GETS PEOPLE

Species: Dermatobia hominis

HABITAT

CLIMATIC ZONE

RATING

Human botflies, as adults, look like small bumblebees and cause harm to no one. But in the larval stage, these opprobrious little maggots can make a monthlong meal out of people, boring through their skin and wandering about their tissues and muscles, munching moderate amounts of them as they go. They sometimes make themselves at home in a hair follicle or some similar bodily recess. For example, they are very fond of nesting in a warm, moist nasal cavity. The adult female botfly has been known to deposit her eggs in a sleeping human's nostrils, particularly someone with a cold, in which case the cold will soon be the least of the victim's worries. As the larvae chew their way through the victim's nasal passages, painful headaches will occur. In some instances, the maggots will eat into the victim's brain and eyes, causing blindness. A rare occurrence in humans, this happens often in sheep—the symptoms are called the blind staggers.

Name/Description

The human botfly, *Dermatobia hominis*, is a hairy, two-winged fly of the family Cuterebridae, found chiefly in Central and South America. As larvae, they are endoparasitic, meaning that they survive in the tissues or organs of a living host, usually a hooved animal but sometimes a human. The adult female botfly frequently enlists the aid of another flying insect to deposit her eggs. In flight, she will fall upon a targeted insect, often a mosquito, and forcibly attach a bundle of about 20 eggs to it. When the carrier insect settles on a warm-blooded animal, it deposits the botfly eggs, which are warmed by the host's body and

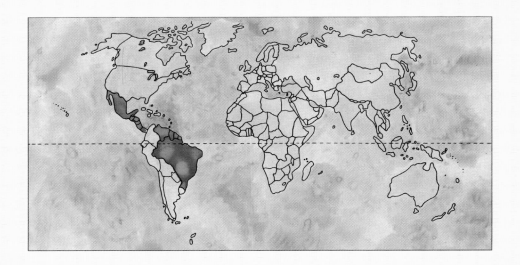

quickly hatch. The larvae slip hastily out of their eggs and immediately dig into the host. After about 40 days, they emerge as inch-long maggots and drop off the host. Pupating in soil, they eventually develop into adult botflies.

Injury/Infection

Human botfly larvae infest open wounds, the eyes, the mouth, the ears, the nasal and genital orifices, the bladder, the trachea, the pulmonary system, or the intestine.

Symptoms

Symptoms of myiasis (fly-maggot infestation) in humans vary greatly, depending on the location and quantity of larvae, and the duration of infestation. Symptoms include festering sores, conjunctivitis, headache, pain and discharge in the ear, nausea, vomiting, abdominal pain, bloody diarrhea, and bloody urine.

Treatment

If the larva is near the surface of the skin it can often be squeezed out, but most have to removed surgically. Larvae in the nasal cavity can be removed by gargling with a strong salt-water solution.

Prevention

- In areas where the botfly is common, avoid sleeping near sheep, horses, or cattle.

Botfly larvae hatched in the human body may eat through the eyes, causing blindness.

Botfly larvae dwell inside their human host and feed for about 40 days before leaving.

JIGGER FLEA

HOW IT GETS PEOPLE

Species: Tunga penetrans

HOW IT GETS PEOPLE

HABITAT

HABITAT

CLIMATIC ZONE

CLIMATIC ZONE

RATING

In the 14th century, when it was called the Black Death, the plague killed 25 million people, one-fourth of the entire population of Europe. This dread disease was transmitted from rats to humans by fleas. Although the plague is not the threat it once was, fleas have yet to shake off their reputation as despicable carriers of disease.

The tiniest of the thousand species of fleas, the chigoe flea (also called the jigger or chigger flea, or the sand flea), does not usually transmit the plague, but it is nevertheless a bloodsucking little pest. Chigoes usually congregate in large groups on the ground and leap onto passing people or animals. Their staple diet is the blood of warm–blooded vertebrates, which they will imbibe daily if possible. The chigoe flea's smooth, hard, streamlined body protects it from the inevitable slapping and scratching of its aggravated host. Because of an extremely rapid digestive process, chigoe fleas can excrete waste as many as 20 times in half an hour, although their huge stomach also allows chigoes to go without food for a year. Thus, chigoes can afford to be picky in choosing their hosts. Often, they choose humans.

Name/Description

For a long time people thought that fleas were grasshoppers without wings, and even today entomologists disagree about their proper clas–sification. Chigoe fleas, of the *Tunga penetrans* species, are wingless, parasitic insects found in tropical parts of the Americas, Asia, and Africa. They are about one twenty–fifth of an inch in length, and are covered with bristles that they use to attach themselves to a host's hair or fur.

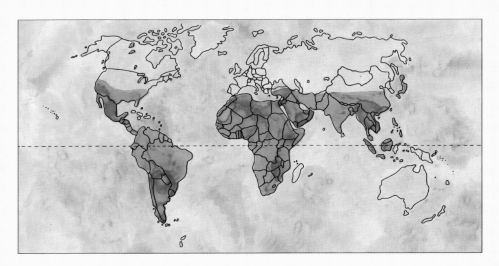

Although they cannot fly, their exoskeleton is especially adapted for leaping. Hungry fleas may jump up to 600 times an hour in search of a host. Chigoe fleas penetrate their host and suck blood with a downward-pointing proboscis. The pregnant female chigoe will burrow head-first into the outer epidermis of a host's skin—often under the toenails or between the toes—and remain there until she is ready to lay her eggs.

Infection/Injury

The chigoe flea is not likely to be a carrier of plague, and its bite is usually painless. But the endoparasitic stage of the female's reproductive cycle can be harmful to a human. When the inseminated female burrows under the epidermis of a human host, she swells to the size of a pea, causing a pus-filled ulcer to form. If the sore becomes infected, gangrene and tetanus can develop.

Symptoms

The ulcerous sore is likely to become infected, resulting in pain, discharge, swelling, itching, fever, and headache. If not treated fairly quickly, an infected toe, foot, or limb may be lost to blood poisoning.

Treatment

Infected sores should be treated by a doctor who will surgically remove the flea, clean and dress the wound, and if necessary prescribe antibiotics. In the West African country of Gabon, one might acquire the services of a certain species of monkey that is quite adept at removing chigoe fleas from human feet and toes.

Prevention

- In infested areas, apply insect repellent to exposed areas of the body every four hours.

A hungry jigger flea may jump up to 600 times in a single hour while in search of a host.

- When hiking in an infested area, wear long trousers and boots that have been saturated with repellent.

- In infested areas, keep possible flea–carriers, such as dogs and other domestic animals, away from tents, houses, and other dwellings.

- In infested areas, inspect yourself thoroughly and frequently.

KILLER BEE

HOW IT GETS PEOPLE

Species: Apis mellifera scutellata

HABITAT

CLIMATIC ZONE

CLIMATIC ZONE

RATING

The hunt was described in an August 1985 issue of *Time* magazine: "In helmets, veils, and heavy gauge cotton overalls, they trudged across the cracked earth of the San Joaquin Valley seeking the killers. Some of the searchers took to the air, combing an area of 400 square miles by helicopter." What were these searchers in their helicopters and strange protective garb looking for? Bees. Killer bees.

The much-publicized killer-bee "invasion" of the Western Hemisphere began in 1956, when 26 African queen bees escaped from a jungle laboratory near São Paulo, Brazil. Since then, the outlaw swarms have expanded and moved steadily northward at a rate of about 200 to 300 miles a year, eventually covering over 7,000 miles in 35 years. In October 1990, U.S. Department of Agriculture scientists intercepted the first swarm of killer bees to fly over the Mexican border. Although the arrival of the bees has been the subject of countless jokes, it is no laughing matter, especially to beekeepers and farmers who find themselves in the path of these ornery, uninvited guests. In California alone, 21 fruit and nut crops and 20 vegetable crops depend on controlled pollination by domestic honeybees. These bees, descendants of the mild–mannered European honeybee, are easily raised and managed by commercial beekeepers, who hire them out as "farmhands" for crop pollination. But once they breed with the newcomers from south of the border, domestic bees inherit the aggressive, uncontrollable characteristics of the killer bees and thus become useless for commercial pollination.

Killer bees pose another, more sinister threat. It is estimated that since their escape from the laboratory in Brazil, the bees have killed about 100 people a year. And it is a terrible way to die. The examination of the body of a University of Miami student killed in Costa Rica in July of 1986 revealed that he had received about 45 killer–bee stings on each square

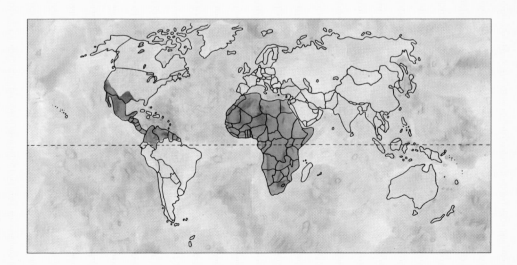

inch of his body. Another victim, who shot himself in agony before the bees could finish him off, was found with 1,000 stings on his head alone.

Name/Description

Killer bees, of the *Apis mellifera scutellata* species, are Africanized New World honeybees. Although they are no more venomous than the ordinary honeybee, killer bees are much quicker to get excited, and once they are angry they stay angry. They live in colonies that can hold as many as 80,000 bees, and woe to the creature that disturbs them, for they attack in giant swarms, pursue a fleeing victim tenaciously, and continue to sting even after their victim is dead.

Toxicology

Killer bees have the same neurotoxins as ordinary honeybees, and although 1 or 2 stings will not seriously harm a nonallergic person, the 400 to 500 stings per minute usually delivered by an attacking killer–bee swarm can kill just about anyone.

Symptoms

Individual stings produce acute local pain, followed by blanching at the site of the sting, which is soon surrounded by an area of redness and irritation. Local nonallergic symptoms usually disappear within 24 hours. (For symptoms of anaphylactic shock, see Hymenoptera Stings, p. 114.)

Treatment

(For treatment of anaphylactic shock, see Hymenoptera Stings, p. 114.)

**A man who received 1,000 killer-bee stings on his head
shot himself to avoid a more agonizing death.**

Prevention

- Can the killer-bee invasion be stemmed? The U.S. Department of Agriculture is currently experimenting with various methods, including
killer-bee traps that use queen-bee scent as a lure, and the government
is offering cash rewards to anyone who locates and reports a killer-bee
hive. But until the killer bee is eradicated, extreme caution should be
exercised by anybody living in or traveling through the affected areas
of South and Central America, southern Texas, and central and southern
California.

KISSING BUG

HOW IT GETS PEOPLE

Species: Reduvius personatus

CLIMATIC ZONE

HABITAT

HABITAT

RATING

The kissing bug—what a charming, romantic name for an insect. But there is nothing charming about this little Cupid, a filthy, cone-nosed vampire that sucks blood from its victims while they sleep. After ingesting 3 to 12 times its own weight in human blood, the engorged kissing bug will add insult to injury by defecating on the sleeping host. This practice is as dangerous as it is revolting, because the fecal matter of the kissing bug carries Chagas' disease, which is at best debilitating and at worst fatal. In some parts of Brazil, where the kissing bug is especially adept at paying nocturnal visits to Brazilians sleeping in hammocks, one-third of adult deaths are attributed to Chagas' disease.

Name/Description

Kissing bugs, also known as assassin bugs, belong to species *Reduvius personatus* of the family Reduviidae and are common in the American tropics. This cousin of the notorious bedbug acquired its sobriquet in 1899 from a much-publicized incident in which a woman was bitten on the lip, or "kissed."

Kissing bugs usually prey on other insects, but they also feed on the fresh blood of some mammals and humans. Hairy, winged larvae that can grow to about an inch in length, kissing bugs disguise themselves as drifting dust balls with a coating of dust and lint, which clings readily to their sticky body. Kissing bugs have a powerful proboscis that is sharp enough to penetrate human skin without awakening the sleeping victim. When threatened, they chirp by scraping the tip of the proboscis over a rippled ridge on the prothorax (the segment connecting the head to the middle section of an insect).

Toxicology

Kissing bugs become carriers of Chagas' disease when they feed upon the blood of an infected person, and they pass on the disease in their feces, which are often inadvertently rubbed into the puncture wound by the scratching of the victims themselves. The disease is caused by minute *Trypanosoma cruzi* organisms, which can, when transmitted into the human bloodstream, damage the heart, the thyroid gland, and the nervous system. Children are especially susceptible.

Symptoms

The bite itself, although usually painless, can produce allergic reactions in sensitive individuals. (For symptoms of anaphylactic shock, see Hymenoptera Stings, p. 114.) Victims who survive allergic symptoms may then have to battle the debilitating effects of Chagas' disease. Symptoms of Chagas' disease may begin with the appearance near the wound of clusters of swollen red eruptions with a central dot of blood, followed by itching and edema (abnormal accumulation of fluid in the tissue) around the wound; prolonged high fever; enlargement of the spleen; the liver, and the lymph nodes; weakness; nausea; and heart palpitations. Long–term complications include permanent damage to internal organs such as the intestines, the liver, and the heart. Symptoms of Chagas' disease can take an inordinate amount of time to develop, and a chance infection from a single exposure, such as a short stopover in an infested tropical area, may go undetected for as long as 20 years.

Treatment

Treatment for Chagas' disease is very difficult because there is no drug available that kills the disease–causing organisms without producing serious side effects in the host. Symptoms of organ damage may be treated symptomatically. (For treatment of anaphylactic shock, see Hymenoptera Stings, p. 114.)

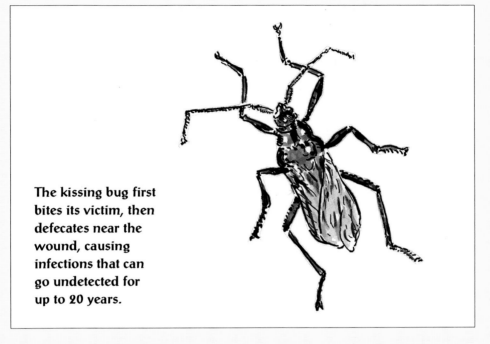

The kissing bug first bites its victim, then defecates near the wound, causing infections that can go undetected for up to 20 years.

Prevention

• While in an infested area, sleep under a secure mosquito net.

• Spray interiors with insecticide.

LYME TICK

HOW IT GETS PEOPLE

Species: Ixodes dammini

RATING

HABITAT

HABITAT

CLIMATIC ZONE

CLIMATIC ZONE

Martha's Vineyard, Nantucket, and Cape Cod are names that bring to mind images of tanned, healthy children on summer holiday, running through grassy fields and tumbling down sand dunes at the beach. But nowadays a threatening shadow looms over these bucolic scenes, and up and down the East Coast of the United States, from the budding of the first jonquil until the forming of the first frost, anxious parents sternly forbid their children from venturing off their manicured lawns into the nearby forests and fields. What terrible creature casts such a long, dark shadow over New England's seashore communities? The Lyme tick, an arachnid parasite no bigger than a pinhead.

The Lyme disease mystery began in the mid–1970s in the small town of Lyme, Connecticut, where an inordinate number of children were suffering from the symptoms of what was thought to be juvenile rheumatoid arthritis. Troubled by this improbable concentration of a rare condition, a task force of researchers, led by Dr. Allen C. Steere of Yale University School of Medicine, came to Lyme and began an investigation. They eventually isolated the disease–causing agent—a corkscrew–shaped microorganism called a spirochete. This spirochete was in turn traced to a species of arachnid, commonly called the deer tick, usually found on field mice and deer. As the investigation continued, the woodlands around Lyme were found to have the highest concentration of deer ticks in the world. The debilitating affliction that these tiny bloodsuckers had been passing on to the bewildered residents of Lyme became known as Lyme disease.

Name/Description

The *Ixodes dammini* species of tick, known as the Lyme or deer tick, is a cousin of the spider. This tiny parasite is much smaller than the common dog tick and is usually carried by field mice and deer, but it can also be found on domestic pets and birds. It has four legs and a miniscule head joined to a rounded body. The deer tick is found throughout the United

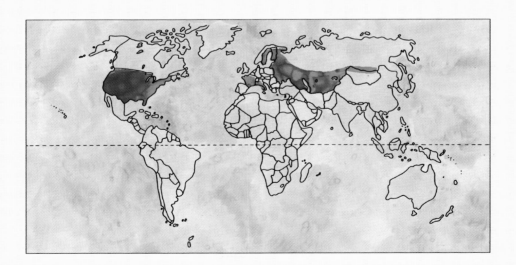

States but is most populous in the Northeast. Female ticks lay up to 8,000 eggs at a time and can sometimes survive for years without food.

Infection/Disease

Lyme disease is caused by the *Borrelia burgdorfer* spirochete, which the deer tick hosts in its stomach. As the tick sucks blood from a person, these spirochetes enter the victim's bloodstream, and the disease process begins.

Symptoms

The biggest problem, especially in areas where the disease is relatively unknown, is correct diagnosis. Unfortunately, in about 30% of Lyme disease cases, there is no warning rash; thus the disease may go untreated until more serious symptoms develop.

In most cases, within 30 days of the tick bite a small bump surrounded by a spreading rash appears near the wound. First-stage symptoms may include headache, fever, enlarged lymph nodes, drowsiness, and other flulike symptoms. Second-stage symptoms, appearing weeks or even months later, include meningitis (inflammation of the membranes that envelope the brain and the spinal cord), paralysis of facial muscles (Bell's palsy), fatigue, headache, stiffness and pain in the joints and muscles, and heart-rhythm abnormalities. Third-stage symptoms, appearing a year or more after the initial infection, are usually arthritic in nature (the knees being most severely affected), but there may also be skin disorders, painful neurological complications, and chronic fatigue.

Treatment

If it is diagnosed soon enough, Lyme disease can be effectively treated with antibiotics such as tetracycline, penicillin, and erythromycin. But

Female Lyme ticks lay up to 8,000 eggs at a time and can sometimes survive for years without food.

without early treatment, second- and third-stage symptoms may develop and linger for months or even years.

Prevention

- If you discover a tick feeding on you, do not panic and pull it violently off, for this may leave you with the tick's head still imbedded in your skin. There are various ways to convince a tick to relax its hold on you. Apply heat from a lit cigarette, candle, or match; smother it with Vaseline; or intoxicate it with alcohol, nail polish remover, or lighter fluid. Then remove it gently with forceps or tweezers and clean the wound carefully.

- If you have been bitten, be on the alert for the distinct circular rash associated with Lyme disease, and seek medical treatment immediately if the rash appears or flulike symptoms develop.

- If you are planning to walk through fields or woodlands in an infested area during tick season (May through July), wear a one-piece garment sprayed with a tick repellent, and keep the pants tucked into socks or boots.

- Inspect yourself, your children, and pets immediately after coming inside.

MANGO FLY

HOW IT GETS PEOPLE

Species: Chrysops dimidiata

HABITAT

CLIMATIC ZONE

RATING

Veterans of travel in the lush equatorial forests of western and central Africa have been known to become particularly unnerved at the ap-pearance of mango flies. It is not the nasty bite of the stout red fly that travelers fear, but rather the hundreds of little stowaways the fly carries with it. These repulsive microfilariae (tiny parasitic worms) are the larvae of the Loa loa worm, and they pass into a human victim's wound via the mango fly's saliva. The worms then begin a five-month grand tour of the human interior that frequently ends at the eyeballs.

Mango Fly

Name/Description

The mango fly (*Chrysops dimidiata*), also known as the tumbu fly, mangrove fly, and red fly, is a large, red, two-winged, biting fly that breeds in shaded African forests. The mango fly is diurnal (most active in the daytime).

Infestation

Loa loa infestation is known as loaiasis. When mango flies bite a person who is already a host, they pick up the Loa loa microfilariae—a single mango fly can carry as many as 200 of these threadlike worms—some of which they will deposit in the puncture wound of their next victim. The worms then begin a burrowing migration beneath the surface of the skin and along the fascial planes (bands of connective tissue deep within the skin), where they sometimes take up permanent residence. Once they have grown large enough—an adult can achieve a length of over two inches—their movements can actually be seen as they travel beneath the host's skin.

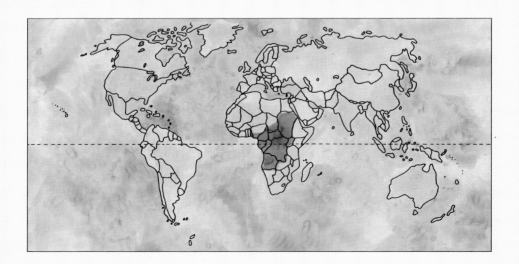

Symptoms

The initial bite of the mango fly causes severe swelling and itching. During the next month, as the microfilariae fan out from their point of entry, papules (small, solid elevations of the skin) may develop. As the invading worms grow and migrate through the human body they leave raised, serpentine tracks on the skin, usually around the victim's back, arms, scrotum, and waist. Known as Calabar swellings, they are terribly irritating and can become numerous and severe enough to incapacitate the victim.

The most dramatic symptoms of loaiasis surface about five months after the initial entry of the microfilariae, when they have grown to adult size. As the full-grown worms move under the skin, the host feels prickling and itching sensations; worms moving deeper within the tissue cause shifting aches and pains. The most horrifying symptoms of all occur if the worms decide to commute across the victim's face. Worms taking this route are clearly visible as they cross the host's eyeballs—a most appalling event.

Treatment

Loaiasis is treatable in the early stages, when the symptoms are not very pronounced. (Unfortunately, many victims attribute these symptoms to a minor skin ailment and do not seek help, and by the time the symptoms become more pronounced it may be too late for effective treatment.) Diethylcarbamazine (DEC) is effective against the microfilariae and also against some of the adult worms, although a proportion of the adult worms will remain resistant to treatment even after repeated doses of DEC.

Ironically, the passage of the worms across a victim's eyeball creates a window of opportunity for treatment. During this migration, which usually lasts for about 30 minutes, the worms are visible and can be removed surgically with little resultant damage to the eye.

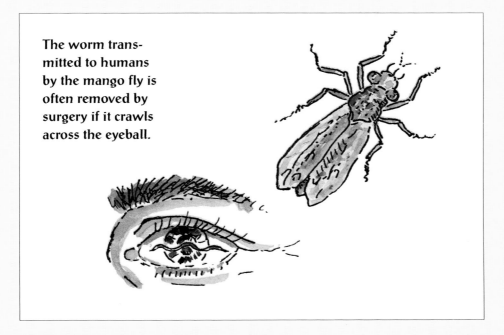

The worm transmitted to humans by the mango fly is often removed by surgery if it crawls across the eyeball.

Prevention

- In infested areas wear trousers and long–sleeved shirts, and apply insect repellent frequently.
- In infested areas, 250–milligram tablets of DEC may be taken for three consecutive days each month as a preventive measure.

POISONOUS
CATERPILLARS

HOW IT GETS PEOPLE

Order: Lepidoptera

HOW IT GETS PEOPLE

HABITAT

HABITAT

CLIMATIC ZONE

RATING

Caterpillars, and especially moth caterpillars, are such cute, furry little creatures that children often spend hours playing with them, placing obstacles in their path for them to crawl over and around, or turning them on their backs to watch as the startled caterpillars try to right themselves. But children should be warned: Hidden within that fuzzy coat is a thicket of short, hollow spines (known as urticating hairs) that have been likened to tiny hypodermic needles—and each is loaded with an irritating toxin.

Name/Description

Caterpillars are the wormlike larvae of the lepidopterans (butterflies and moths). Ranging in size from three-quarters of an inch to three and a quarter inches, their shape and coloration vary from species to species, and they feed, for the most part, on a variety of plants. Poisonous caterpillar species are found in Europe, North America, Africa, and Asia, and they include the puss caterpillar, the brown-tail moth caterpillar, the gypsy moth caterpillar, the hag moth caterpillar, the buck moth caterpillar, and two of the most striking caterpillars—the saddleback caterpillar and the io moth caterpillar. The saddleback caterpillar's sluglike body is marked with a brown or purplish "saddle" on a green or white "saddle blanket." The long, pale-green io moth caterpillar is marked with stripes of red or maroon over white that run the length of its body.

Injury/Toxicology

Caterpillar poisonings are very common. During one summer in Texas there were 2,130 reported caterpillar stings. The toxic principles of

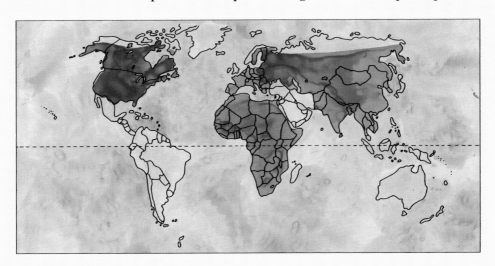

caterpillar poison are unknown, but it is very easy to come into contact with the poison in an infested area. The caterpillar's hollow spines break on contact with a victim's skin, allowing the toxin to flow out of the spines and into the wound. Although children frequently get stung while handling the caterpillars, most poisonings are the result of casual, inadvertent contact with the larvae or even with infested vegetation. Airborne spines can also get in the eyes or be inhaled.

Symptoms

Contact with a poisonous caterpillar will cause immediate burning pain, followed by local numbness and swelling, with radiating pain. Unremoved spines can produce pustules. (If an io moth caterpillar crawls across your skin a track of parallel red puncture marks will be left behind.) Sometimes there is swelling of regional lymph nodes downstream (toward the heart) from the site of contact. Symptoms of severe poisoning include nausea, vomiting, high fever, headache, shock, and convulsions. Urticating hairs in the eyes can cause conjunctivitis. Inhalation of hairs may cause irritation, inflammation, and pain in the throat and lungs, as well as allergic reactions.

Treatment

Try to remove all the imbedded hairs from the victim's skin by repeated application of adhesive tape. Ice packs and a paste of baking soda and water should be applied to the irritated areas.

Prevention

- Cover up when working outside in an infested area; wear gloves, a long-sleeved shirt, and long pants.
- Many poisonings occur when victims put on washed clothing that has been hung out to dry and that has subsequently become infested; inspect all such clothing before you put it on.

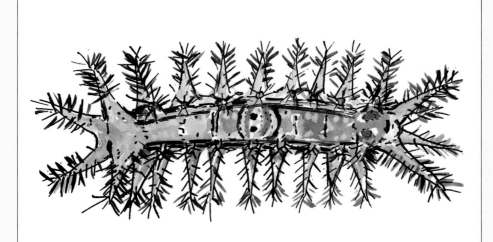

The poisonous hairs found on many caterpillars have been likened to hypodermic needles.

- Warn children not to play with or touch caterpillars.
- Spray infested vegetation with an appropriate insecticide.

POLISTES WASP

HOW IT GETS PEOPLE

Family: Vespidae

HABITAT

CLIMATIC ZONE

CLIMATIC ZONE

RATING

Actually, it was not a spider that frightened Little Miss Muffet, but an angry horde of wasps. According to the recently discovered diary of Dr. T. Muffet, writer of the famous nursery rhyme and father of Miss Patience Muffet, the episode that inspired the rhyme occurred during an outing in England's Epping Forest, when the Muffets were forced to flee from a swarm of wasps who wanted to share their picnic. So why did an innocent spider take the blame for scaring Miss Muffet? Probably because *spider* rhymes better with *sat down beside her*.

Poliste Wasp

Nursery rhymes and spiders aside, Dr. Muffet and his little girl certainly did the right thing when they decided to abandon their picnic baskets to the wasps. In the United States, wasps, including the members of the *Polistes* genus, kill more people annually than do snakes, scorpions, and poisonous spiders combined. And many deaths caused by wasps are not included in the official statistics because they are so often mistakenly attributed to causes such as cardiac failure or heatstroke. Wasp attacks are also responsible for an untold number of fatal car accidents.

Name/Description

Polistes wasps are social members of the family Vespidae. This cousin of the hornet is found worldwide. *Polistes* wasps have smooth, hard, stalk-waisted bodies with well-developed wings and powerful mandibles. Only the female *Polistes* stings; her stinger has no barbs, so she can sting a victim repeatedly. From one-half an inch to an inch long, the female is chocolate colored, whereas the males are liberally splashed with yellow on their faces and legs, and they have yellow rings encircling

their body. *Polistes* wasps hatch from eggs and undergo a complete metamorphosis, including larval and pupal stages, culminating in adult-hood as a fully grown wasp.

Toxicology

The female *Polistes* wasp's stinger is a modified ovipositor (the tubelike organ through which the female deposits her eggs). *Polistes* wasps have an alkaline venom containing enzymes and hemolytic (red blood-cell destroying) agents. The venom also functions as a neurotoxin and a vasodilator (an agent causing a widening of blood vessel openings).

Symptoms

The sting will feel like a sharp pinprick followed by a burning pain. The initial pain usually subsides within a few hours and may be followed by itching, swelling, and aches. But these immediate reactions are not the only ones to be feared, for there are symptoms that may not manifest themselves for up to two years. Although it has long been known that wasp stings can cause severe bleeding and damage to the kidneys and blood vessels, physicians are now finding that they may also damage the brain, the spinal cord, and the nerves. (For symptoms of anaphylactic reaction, see Hymenoptera Stings, p. 114.)

Treatment

Wash the area around the sting with soap and water. Ice or a cold towel will soothe the burning sensation and prevent swelling. (For treatment of anaphylactic reaction, see Hymenoptera Stings, p. 114.)

Prevention

• The female *Polistes* wasp builds a simple home—a papery, unenclosed, honeycombed nest suspended from a short stem. Looking like tiny

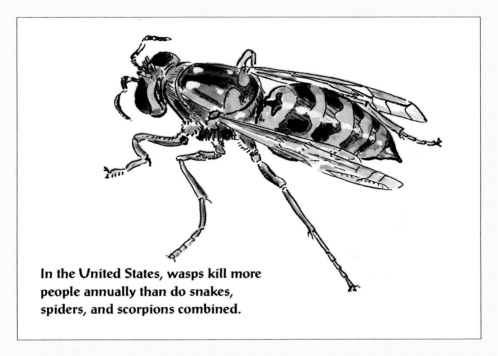

In the United States, wasps kill more people annually than do snakes, spiders, and scorpions combined.

umbrellas, the nests are usually found on trees, under shed or barn roofs, and under the eaves of houses. If you discover one, do not attempt to remove it. Call an exterminator. (For prevention of anaphylactic reaction, see Hymenoptera Stings, p. 114.)

ROCKY MOUNTAIN WOOD TICK

Species: Dermacentor andersoni

HOW IT GETS PEOPLE

CLIMATIC ZONE

HABITAT

RATING

People like to think that they know their own body, so a certain apprehension is natural when someone notices an alien little bump on their scalp or neck. If that bump turns out to be a tick, its mouth firmly embedded in their skin and its body bloated with their blood, apprehension quickly turns to revulsion. And, if they are aware of the possible consequences of a tick bite—fever, paralysis, and even death—revulsion may be followed by outright fear.

Name/Description

The Rocky Mountain wood tick, *Dermacentor andersoni*, found primarily in the Rocky Mountain regions of the United States, is a tiny, wingless parasite belonging to the Ixodoidea superfamily of arachnids. Female wood ticks are dark red in color; males are a grayish white. These ticks, especially the females, are voracious bloodsuckers. During one meal, the female can increase her size eightfold.

86

After her banquet, she will drop off of her host (talk about eating and running!), and then deposit 4,000 to 7,000 eggs in an elongated mass. A few weeks later she will die. But her many offspring will hatch and eventually develop into adult parasites, victimizing various animals and humans as well. For human hosts, the actual bite and parasitization process are relatively painless and harmless. But the diseases that the tick might transmit to the host during this period are not.

Injury/Toxicology

The Rocky Mountain wood tick can transmit three extremely dangerous diseases to human hosts. If the tick attaches itself to the back of the neck or the base of the skull for a week or more, it can cause a mysterious and frightening condition known as tick paralysis. Scientists believe that this condition is caused by a toxic substance introduced into the host by the tick during feeding.

Rocky Mountain wood ticks also carry tularemia, also known as rabbit fever or deerfly fever. Tularemia is caused by the *Pasteurella tularensis* bacterium, which the tick transmits from animal hosts to humans.

The most serious disease transmitted by the Rocky Mountain wood tick is the dreaded Rocky Mountain spotted fever, which is also carried by dog ticks and lone star ticks in areas outside the Rocky Mountains. Rocky Mountain spotted fever is caused by the *Rickettsia rickettsii* microorganism, which is also transmitted by the tick from animals to humans. First identified in the 1890s in Montana, this disease is found in all but nine states, although 80% of the cases now occur east of the Mississippi River.

Symptoms

Symptoms of tick paralysis include lethargy, muscle weakness, incoor-dination, nystagmus (involuntary, rapid eye movement), and paralysis of the motor nerves affecting first the legs, then, a few days later, the arms, and gradually spreading, if unchecked, until there is total paralysis and death.

Symptoms of tularemia include small pimples at the site of the bite that develop into festering sores, lesions on the fingers, hands, eyes, or mouth, followed by headache, chills, nausea, vomiting, high fever, and prostration.

The first symptoms of Rocky Mountain spotted fever appear 3 to 12 days after the initial tick bite. They include a rash characterized by the appearance of rose-colored spots on the hands, wrists, feet, and ankles, which then spread over the entire body, turning the skin a violet color. Ensuing symptoms include chills, severe headache, muscle aches, pros-tration, loss of appetite, nausea, coughing, vomiting, high fever, fluid retention, conjunctivitis, mental confusion, and shortness of breath. Untreated, Rocky Mountain spotted fever can cause pneumonia, tissue necrosis, circulatory failure, brain and heart damage, and death.

Treatment

Tick paralysis can usually be alleviated by prompt removal of the tick, although respiratory assistance may be needed in the interim.

Bloodsucking ticks generally remain anchored to their host for one to two weeks.

For tularemia, streptomycin should be administered until the body temperature is normal; gentamycin has also proven effective. Continuous wet saline dressings are beneficial for skin lesions, although large abscesses may have to be drained.

Because of the wide variety of symptoms, Rocky Mountain spotted fever is difficult to diagnose. If Rocky Mountain spotted fever is suspected, blood tests should be taken as soon as possible. Early detection is essential to successful treatment with antibiotics (tetracycline and chloramphenicol).

Prevention

- During tick season, while outdoors wear a one–piece garment tucked into your boots.

- Conduct frequent body and scalp searches. (For tick removal, see Lyme Tick, p. 70.)

- Apply tick repellent frequently.

- If you are in a heavily infested area you may want to try a new vaccine for Rocky Mountain spotted fever, which provides immunity with the aid of seasonal booster injections.

SAND FLY

HOW IT GETS PEOPLE

Species: Phlebotomus papatasii

RATING

HABITAT

HABITAT

HABITAT

HABITAT

CLIMATIC ZONE

CLIMATIC ZONE

For many, to visit Mayan ruins such as Palenque or Chichén Itzá is a lifelong dream. But for those who actually travel to these places in the humid lowlands of Mexico, Belize, and Guatemala, the dream can become a nightmare, for it is in those regions that the hated sand fly flourishes. One of the world's most annoying pests, the tiny, mothlike sand fly must also be one of the filthiest. In its quest for a hot, humid atmosphere, it inhabits sewers, outhouses, and rubbish dumps. One of its preferred environments is a post-earthquake pile of rubble. So tiny that it can easily pass through mosquito nets and window screens, the sand fly is most active during the still hours around dawn and dusk, when there is no breeze to blow it off course. And a dawn or twilight visit from this pest can leave a person sick, disfigured—or dead.

Name/Description

Sand flies, *Phlebotomus papatasii*, are compact biting flies of the family Psychodidae, common to tropical regions around the world. The sand fly resembles a tiny moth, having a hairy body and two woolly wings. Sand fly larvae require a hot, humid atmosphere and usually inhabit putrid sites where they feed on bacteria. Adult sand flies have a piercing-sucking proboscis used to extract blood from victims.

Infection

The sand fly transmits diseases by sucking the blood of an infected individual and then infecting a new host during a subsequent meal. The

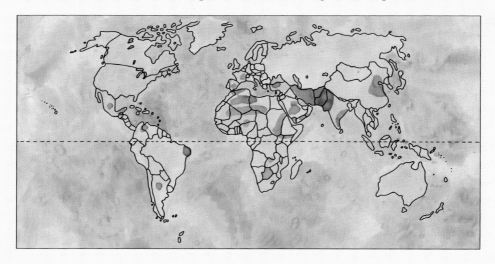

most common of these diseases is the short–term viral infection known as sand–fly fever, or phlebotomus fever. Sand flies also carry and transmit two forms of leishmaniasis—cutaneous leishmaniasis and visceral leishmaniasis.

Symptoms

Symptoms of sand–fly fever are flulike in nature. They include headache, fever, sweating, chills, muscle aches and pains, and fatigue, and they usually pass within a few days. Symptoms of cutaneous leishmaniasis are more serious and more permanent. The various names given to this condition in various parts of the world—chiclero ulcer, Oriental sore, Baghdad boil, Biskra button—all reflect its most characteristic symptom: unsightly skin ulcerations that usually affect the face. These symptoms can result in permanent scarring. Left untreated, cutaneous leishmaniasis can eat away at a victim's extremities in an almost leprous fashion.

Cutaneous leishmaniasis can disfigure you, but visceral leishmaniasis can kill you. Symptoms of visceral leishmaniasis, or kala–azar, may develop soon after the bite or as long as two years later. They include prolonged fever, enlargement of the spleen and liver, anemia, and severe weight loss. Death can result if the disease is left untreated.

Treatment

Specific treatment for sand–fly fever is not necessary, as the symptoms usually disappear within three days. An analgesic should relieve any discomfort. For cutaneous leishmaniasis, antimony drugs are effective. One of the major problems in correct diagnosis of visceral leishmaniasis is the delay between the initial infection and the onset of symptoms, which often leads to misdiagnosis. Once it has been correctly identified, visceral leishmaniasis can be successfully treated with the antimony drug Pentostam.

In parts of the Middle East and Brazil, entire communities suffer from the leprosylike diseases spread by the sand fly.

Prevention

- While in an infested area, cover as much skin as possible during the hours around dawn and dusk.

- In the Middle Eastern regions, do not camp near the burrows of wild gerbils, which usually attract sand flies.

- If you must sleep outside, try to sleep on an elevated platform such as a roof; the breeze will keep the sand flies away.

- Children, who are especially susceptible to leishmaniasis, should sleep under a sand–fly net, which has a very tiny mesh.

- Apply and continually reapply insect repellent.

SCABIES ITCH MITE

HOW IT GETS PEOPLE

Species: *Sarcoptes scabiei*

HABITAT

CLIMATIC ZONE

CLIMATIC ZONE

RATING

In medieval times, the well–equipped traveler often brought a few pigs along for the journey. Arriving at a roadside inn for the night, the wayfarer would deposit the pig in his or her bed before going to dinner, in the hope that all the vermin left behind in the bed by previous lodgers would satisfy their appetite on the pig. Theoretically, the traveler could then enjoy an unmolested night's rest. And, if the pig had done its job, the traveler would not have to worry about a sudden manifestation of a torturous condition known as "the itch" somewhere down the road.

Also known as the seven-year itch, this affliction is caused by tiny creatures known as scabies itch mites. Different species of itch mite are named for their preferred host—*Sarcoptes scabiei hominis* (human itch mite), *S.s. equi* (horse itch mite), *S.s. bovis* (cow itch mite), and *S.s. cameli* (camel itch mite)—but they are all most unwelcome wherever they go.

Name/Description

Itch mites, *Sarcoptes scabiei*, are minute, oval-shaped, specialized relatives of the spider and the scorpion. Found worldwide, itch mites are barely visible to the human eye. Their skin is pale and lined like the human palm, with rough, scattered spines in some places. Itch mites have no true head, but they do have four pairs of legs, some of which end in suckers.

Infection/Infestation

Scabies is a skin condition caused by human itch-mite infestation. Itch mites are easily transmitted from one infested person to another

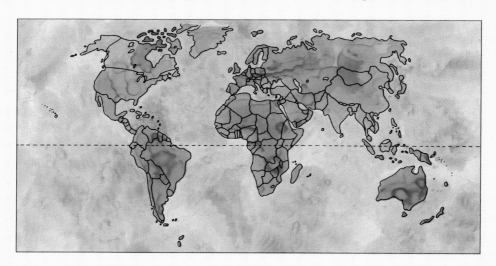

through casual contact or contact with infested clothing, sheets, towels etc. Upon arrival on a new human host, the minuscule mite will tunnel through the outer layers of the host's skin, preferring soft and wrinkled areas such as the spaces between fingers and toes, the forearms and wrists, the armpits, the navel, and the genitals and buttocks.

Itch mites mate on, or in, their host; the male then dies, and the female burrows into the skin to make a tunnel in which to lay her eggs. Within four or five days, the 25 to 30 eggs will hatch, and the young mites will go tunneling off to mate and repeat the whole process, which only takes a few weeks. It has been estimated that a single pair of itch mites may give rise to 1 million offspring within three months—a very itchy prospect indeed.

Symptoms

All this tunneling, feeding, mating, mothering, and egg–hatching causes an intolerable itching that even the most stoic cannot help but scratch violently. Because warmth stimulates the activity of the mites, sleep often becomes impossible for the host. If the condition is left untreated, a rash may develop. Continued scratching can lead to open sores, inflammation, and deep skin infection. The subsequent lesions may become very extensive and resemble impetigo or eczema. The tunneling of the pregnant mite raises tiny, gray, linear elevations (actually the roofs of the tunnels) on the host's skin. Small blisters may form at tunnel entrances. Once a sensitivity to scabies has been established, any contact with itch mites, even years later, will cause an almost immediate recurrence.

Treatment

Itch–mite infestation and scabies are easily treated with benzyl benzoate cream. A single treatment will usually eliminate the infestation, but a

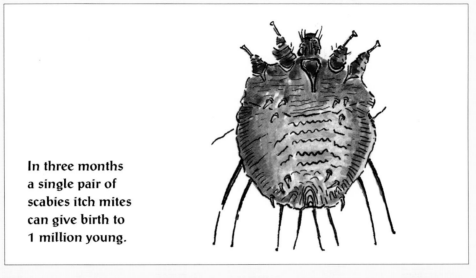

In three months a single pair of scabies itch mites can give birth to 1 million young.

second may sometimes be necessary a week later. All clothing, bedding, and towels used by the infested person should be fumigated, and he or she should be quarantined until mite-free.

Prevention

• Maintain strict personal hygiene and avoid contact with individuals who might be harboring these fugitive, itchy mites.

SCORPION

HOW IT GETS PEOPLE

Order: Scorpionida

RATING

HABITAT

HABITAT

CLIMATIC ZONE

CLIMATIC ZONE

For every person killed in Mexico by poisonous snakes, 10 are killed by scorpions. The nasty Durango scorpion (named for the Mexican town where it was discovered), was responsible for 1,608 fatalities between 1895 and 1926. Most of the victims were children. When a bounty was offered for Durangos, 100,000 were turned in during a three-month period. From the desert area around Phoenix, Arizona, St. Luke's Hospital received 1,400 victims of scorpion stings in a year. The North African species, *Androctonus australis*, poisoned 20,164 people in southern Algeria during a 17-year period. Near Bombay, India, a "casual hunt" for scorpions revealed that nearly 15,000 scorpions lived in an area inhabited by only 13,000 people.

Name/Description

The Scorpionida are an order of primitive arachnids found in hot and tropical regions around the world. Scorpions are characterized by a flattened, elongated body (for hiding in cracks) ending in a segmented telson (a stinging spine, or tail). At the tip of the telson are paired venom glands. The scorpion has 8 legs, 2 to 12 eyes, depending on the species, and 2 large chelae, or claws. Scorpions range in length from one–half inch to nine inches (although a monstrous 11–inch scorpion was once captured in West Bengal, India).

Scorpions are solitary hunting arachnids that feed primarily on other insects. They are extremely hostile to other scorpions; when two adults are seen together, they are either mating or fighting to the death, and female scorpions have been known to devour males after mating. Baby scorpions ride around on their mother's back until their first molting (shedding of skin), after which they become independent. Some scorpions have been known to live for as long as five years.

Toxicology

The scorpion's stinging telson is usually only brought into use for self–defense or to kill difficult prey. The scorpion delivers its sting by curling the telson over its back and then quickly and accurately striking

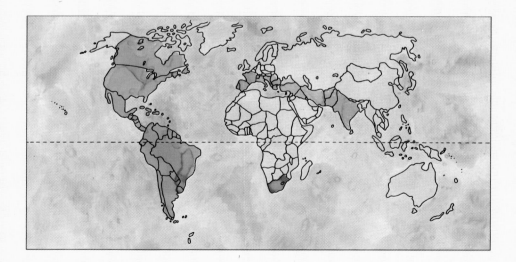

the tip into the victim, sometimes more than once. The venom is neurotoxic, cardiotoxic (affecting the heart), and hemolytic (red blood–cell destroying). The strength of the venom varies greatly with the species; the sting of some scorpions will only produce flulike symptoms in a human victim; the venom of others, like the Durango scorpion or the Sahara scorpion, can kill a person within an hour. The most venomous are the straw-colored scorpions of the genus *Centuroides*. Arachnid expert David Harbster asserts that you can easily distinguish the *Centuroides* scorpions by examining their subaculear tubercle—a little bump under its stinger—but who wants to risk getting close enough to do that?

Symptoms

All scorpion stings are very painful. In the case of a mild envenomization, the site of the sting will be red with some local swelling and pain. There may also be vomiting, diarrhea, sweating, difficulty in swallowing, pale skin, and excess salivation. In the case of severe envenomization, there will be sharp burning at the site of the sting, swelling, sweating, restlessness, horripilation (prickling sensations accompanied by goose flesh and bristling hair), excess salivation, confusion, bloody diarrhea and vomiting, abdominal pain, chest pain, numbness, muscular twitching, respiratory distress, and convulsions. The victim usually remains conscious during this time and experiences a sensation of anguish and depression. Death is caused by respiratory paralysis, and may occur within a few minutes or not until 30 hours after the sting. A false recovery, followed by total relapse, is common. Children are highly susceptible to scorpion venom. In victims under five years old there is a 25% mortality rate.

Treatment

A specific scorpion antivenin is available, and there are also reports of prompt symptomatic relief from the use of the drug chlorpromazine. For

The scorpion is the oldest existing land animal and could probably survive a nuclear holocaust.

intense pain a powerful analgesic, such as pethidine, may be given via intramuscular injection. (Meperidine and morphine, however, are not advised for a scorpion sting, and their use in a scorpion sting victim could prove fatal.)

Prevention

- Normally nonaggressive, scorpions will readily sting when threatened or cornered—and especially when stepped or sat upon. In infested areas, look carefully around tent flaps, in clothing, towels, shoes, and bed–covers.

- When you are outside, look before you sit and do not go barefoot.

TARANTULA

HOW IT GETS PEOPLE

Family: Theraphosidae

RATING

HABITAT

HABITAT

HABITAT

HABITAT

CLIMATIC ZONE

CLIMATIC ZONE

This Store Patrolled By Tarantulas, the sign in the window of the San Francisco jewelry store read. And indeed, passersby who looked in the window could see the hand-sized monsters stalking among the pearl necklaces and diamond rings in the showcases. Plagued by a series of burglaries, the owner of the store had decided to employ the spiders as "watchdogs." As soon as the tarantulas had been installed, the thefts ceased. It seemed that no burglar, no matter how daring or desperate, was willing to risk a confrontation with those fearsome creatures.

Tarantula

Name/Description

The term *tarantula* commonly refers to various species of large, hairy spiders of the Theraphosidae family, found in tropical regions through-out the world. Tarantulas are the world's largest spiders. Some of the massive, tree–dwelling tarantulas of South America have been known to develop leg spans of up to 11 inches. These monsters dine on birds, frogs, and other small animals; smaller species eat insects. All of the tarantulas are solitary hunting spiders. Their long legs allow them to move with alarming quickness, and they use curved, tusklike fangs to seize and poison their victims. When threatened, the tarantula rears up on its four hind legs and presents its fangs to the aggressor—a truly intimidating sight. Tarantulas can have a lifespan of 10 years or more.

Toxicology

Tarantulas are undoubtedly the most frightening of spiders. But their true nature is not equal to their terrifying appearance, for most of them

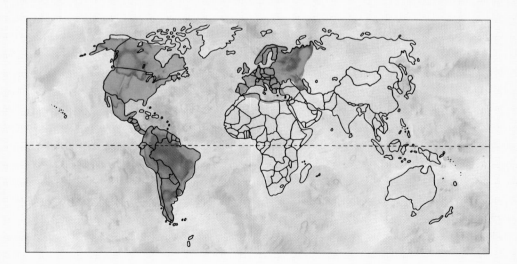

are unaggressive and only mildly venomous, and certain species such as the orange–kneed Mexican tarantula are so docile that they have become popular as pets. Native American children in the southwestern United States actually keep their pet tarantulas on leashes! Although the red–legged South American *Lycosa phoneutria* species is thought to be hostile and dangerously venomous, most tarantulas will not bite a human unless provoked. Their bite is painful, but the venom is thought to be a relatively harmless neurotoxin. The primary danger is the possibility of a severe allergic reaction.

Symptoms

A tarantula bite will hurt more or less like the sting of a honeybee. Usually there is only a local inflammation that lasts a few hours; sometimes this will be accompanied by itching and muscle spasms. Necrosis (dying skin) may occur around the bite. Some species have been known to use their rear legs to flick hairs at intruders or tormentors; these hairs can be very irritating. There have been rare cases of severe allergic reaction to tarantula bites. (For symptoms of anaphylactic shock, see Hymenoptera Stings, p. 114.)

Treatment

Tarantula bites should be treated like wasp or bee stings. There is a specific antivenin available for *Lycosa phoneutria*. (For treatment of anaphylactic shock, see Hymenoptera Stings, p. 114.)

Prevention
• Do not provoke.

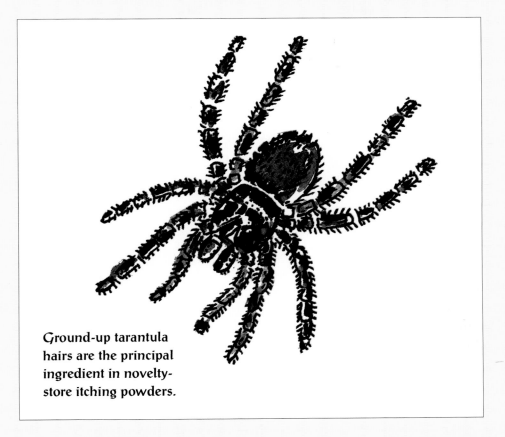

Ground-up tarantula hairs are the principal ingredient in novelty-store itching powders.

TSETSE FLY

HOW IT GETS PEOPLE

Genus: Glossina

CLIMATIC ZONE

HABITAT

HABITAT

RATING

"Their sleeps are sound and sense of feeling very little; for pulling, clubbing or whipping will scarcely stir up sense and power enough to move; and down they fall again into a state of insensibility." Thus did a British surgeon describe the debilitating symptoms of African sleeping sickness, or trypanosomiasis, a disease that can reduce its doomed victims to a zombielike state before they finally sink into an irreversible coma. The English physician observed these symptoms in 1720; in the last decade there have been major sleeping-sickness epidemics in Cameroon, Uganda, and Zaire, and today, at least 25,000 people in Africa are infected annually. The agent of infection is the tsetse fly, a gluttonous parasite that can drink twice its own weight in blood during a single meal.

Name/Description

The tsetse fly is a two-winged biting fly found only in Africa. There are 22 different species of tsetse flies belonging to the genus *Glossina*; each has specific requirements in terms of habitat and host. A little larger than the common horsefly, the tsetse fly breeds along rivers and streams, is active during the day, and feeds exclusively on fresh mammalian blood. The adult flies transmit trypanosomiasis, an infection of the central nervous system commonly known as sleeping sickness.

Infection

Trypanosomiasis is caused by trypanosomes, microorganisms that the tsetse fly carries in its saliva and passes on to its host during feeding.

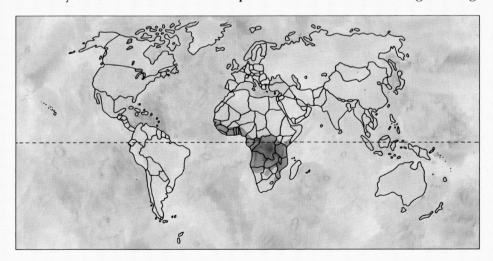

There are two forms of trypanosomiasis, Rhodesian and Gambian. Rhodesian trypanosomiasis, also known as nagana, is primarily trans- mitted from animal to animal, although humans who live near wild animals such as the bushbuck are also subject to infection. The much more prevalent Gambian form of trypanosomiasis only affects humans and is transmitted from person to person by tsetse flies.

Symptoms

If a tsetse fly lands on you, inserts its proboscis into your skin, and begins to suck, you probably will not notice, for the fly injects a local anesthetic while it feeds, thus preventing you from feeling any pain and attempting to interrupt its dinner. Symptoms of both the Gambian and Rhodesian forms of trypanosomiasis are similar, except that the latter develops much more rapidly and is more virulent, usually causing death within four months.

Once the fly's anesthetic wears off, the victim will feel itching and irritation around the bite, frequently accompanied by a deep-red boil- like lesion, which may become quite large. About five days later there will be an onset of fever, headache, lethargy, and swelling of the neck and other glands. These symptoms will recur at irregular intervals of a few days or weeks. If the disease remains untreated, the victim will experience reduced resistance to other diseases, drastic weight loss, loss of ambition and vitality, profound weakness and lethargy, an inability to stay awake, and finally, coma and death.

Treatment

In 18th-century British colonial days, the recommended treatment for sleeping sickness was a quick plunge in the ocean, or a pinch of snuff. Today there are several antiparasitic drugs—such as suramin and pen- tamidine—that have proven effective for both the treatment of infection

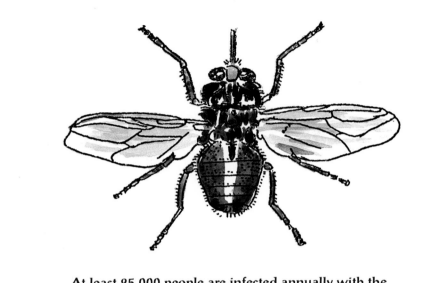

At least 25,000 people are infected annually with the tsetse fly–borne sleeping sickness.

and the prevention of reinfection. In advanced cases melarsoprol may be administered, but only under careful supervision because of its toxicity.

Prevention

- Tsetse flies are attracted by large, moving objects, smells, and navy–blue coloring. In an infested region, travelers should avoid navy–blue clothing or other materials, such as tents, and should apply liberally a suitable insect repellent.

- Wear long trousers and long–sleeved shirts in colors that blend in with the background.

VAMPIRE FLY

HOW IT GETS PEOPLE

Species: *Simulium damnosum*

HABITAT

CLIMATIC ZONE

CLIMATIC ZONE

CLIMATIC ZONE

RATING

True to its name, the vampire fly drinks human blood. But the vampire fly does not just lance the skin like a mosquito; it chews, gnaws, and then sucks up the resulting soup through its proboscis. The bite of this vampire will not turn you into one of the undead, but it might leave you with a horrific condition known as river blindness. The extraordinary

19th-century explorer Mary Kingsley described a "lovely case" of river blindness thusly: "The entire white of one eye [was] full of active little worms and a ridge of surplus population [was] migrating across the bridge of the nose onto the other eye, looking like the bridge of a pair of spectacles." River blindness is most common in Africa, where there are villages in which almost every adult is sightless; the children have to act as guides, leading the adults about. Sometimes children are also infected—in the village of Kouloum only about 20% of the children have normal eyesight. Seventeen million people are currently suffering from river blindness.

Name/Description

The vampire fly, *Simulium damnosum*, a cousin of the hated buffalo gnat, is found in various climates and environments—including the Arctic—around the world. It resembles the common blackfly and feeds exclusively on blood. Vampire flies spend their larval and pupal stages in flowing water, and are therefore populous around rivers and streams.

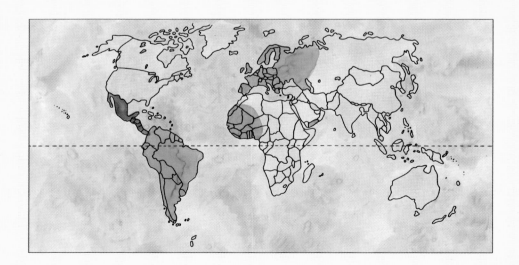

Dangerous Insects

The vampire fly transmits onchocerciacis, or river blindness, which is prevalent in West Africa as well as in parts of Latin America and the Middle East.

Infection

As the vampire fly goes from meal to bloody meal, it transmits to its hosts microscopic worms (*Onchocerca volvulus*), which can live for up to 18 years in the host. Circulating in the blood of the host, these microfilariae eventually infest the eyes, causing lesions and ultimately total blindness.

Symptoms

Symptoms of onchocerciasis may not appear for 12 or more years after infestation. The primary initial symptom will be the appearance of small nodules on the outer skin and in the subcutaneous tissue, accompanied by intense itching and necrosis. When the worms reach the eye, where they can easily be seen by an outside observer, they cause ocular lesions that grow and coalesce, followed by inflammation of the cornea and retina, and finally blindness.

Treatment

Onchocerca microfilariae are killed by ivermectin, given orally after meals. An antihistamine and prednisone may be administered to prevent the acute allergic inflammation in and around the eye that follows the rapid destruction of numerous microfilariae. Adult worms are eliminated by surgical removal.

Prevention

• In heavily infected areas, wear long shirts, trousers, and socks.
• Use that insect repellent!

In some African towns the entire adult population has been blinded by a vampire fly–transmitted parasite.

HYMENOPTERA STINGS

The hymenopterans are a specialized order of biting or stinging insects that undergo complete metamorphosis and that usually possess four membranous wings. The hymenopterans include wasps, hornets, bees, and ants, and they are responsible for the majority of stings—and subsequent allergic reactions—inflicted by insects on humans. For a nonallergic victim, a sting by an angry hymenopteran can be a minor, if somewhat painful, annoyance. But for someone who is sensitive to the insect's toxin, it can be a harrowing and potentially life–threatening event.

Symptoms of Mild Reactions

The sting or bite usually feels like a hard pinprick and is followed by a painful burning sensation. A red area about two inches in diameter forms around the sting. In a few hours the pain subsides and may be followed by itching, soreness, and localized swelling.

Treatment for Mild Reactions

Remove the stinger or stinger fragments, preferably with a dull knife or clean fingernail. Wash the wound with soap and water and apply ice or calamine lotion to soothe the stinging. Then cover the wound and elevate the affected extremity for an hour or so. If necessary, administer acetaminophen to reduce swelling.

Symptoms of Anaphylactic Reactions

Anaphylactic reactions to the sting or bite of a hymenopteran occur in individuals who are highly sensitive, or allergic, to the insect's toxin. In the United States alone more than 2 million people—mostly adults—are susceptible to anaphylaxis; those who have had an anaphylactic reaction once have a 60% chance of recurrence.

Anaphylactic symptoms include wheezing, coughing, sneezing, stomach pain, dizziness, and itching. As the reaction progresses, the victim may experience hives, nausea, vomiting, confusion, weakness, agitation, difficulty in breathing and swallowing, thickened speech caused by swelling of the lips, tongue, and throat, and diarrhea. Untreated, the victim may succumb to anaphylactic shock and die of respiratory failure.

Treatment of Anaphylactic Reactions

Anaphylactic reactions can be relieved with epinephrine and other antihistamines, although a patient in acute respiratory distress may require a tracheotomy (surgical opening of the trachea, or windpipe). Victims with severe reactions should remain in the hospital long enough to ensure adequate treatment in case of relapse, which is fairly common.

Prevention of Hymenoptera Bites and Stings

If you are in an area where you are likely to encounter hymenopterans—which is just about anywhere in the summer—when outdoors, cover foods and beverages, stay away from garbage areas, wear light-colored clothing, avoid wearing perfumes, deodorants, and hairsprays, and do not go barefoot. If hymenopterans approach, do not make sudden movements.

If you have suffered a previous anaphylactic reaction, wear a Medic–alert, or similar bracelet or necklace, and carry an emergency self-treatment kit, such as Ana–kit (available with a doctor's prescription), especially when camping or hiking. The best prevention is a course of immunotherapy injections, which are extremely effective.

FURTHER READING

Askew, R. R. *Parasitic Insects*. London: Heinemann, 1971.

Ballentine, Bill. *Nobody Loves a Cockroach*. Boston: Little, Brown, 1967.

Caras, Roger A. *Dangerous to Man*. South Hackensack, NJ: Stoeger, 1975.

Comstock, John Henry. *The Spider Book*. London: Comstock, 1978.

Hellman, Hal. *Deadly Bugs and Killer Insects*. New York: Evans, 1978.

O'Toole, Christopher, ed. *The Encyclopedia of Insects*. New York: Facts on File, 1968.

Preston–Mafham, Rod, and Ken Preston–Mafham. *Spiders of the World*. New York: Facts on File, 1984.

Ritchie, Carson I. A. *Insects, the Creeping Conquerors*. New York: Elsevier/Nelson Books, 1979.

Rood, Ronald. *It's Going to Sting Me*. New York: Simon & Schuster, 1976.

Wootton, Anthony. *Insects of the World*. New York: Facts on File, 1984.

INDEX

Missy Allen is a writer and photographer whose work has appeared in *Time, Geo, Vogue, Paris-Match, Elle*, and many European publications. Allen holds a master's degree in education from Boston University. Before her marriage to Michel Peissel, she worked for the Harvard School of Public Health and was director of admissions at Harvard's Graduate School of Arts and Sciences.

Michel Peissel is an anthropologist, explorer, inventor, and author. He has studied at the Harvard School of Business, Oxford University, and the Sorbonne. Called "the last true adventurer of the 20th century," Peissel discovered 14 Mayan sites in the eastern Yucatán at the age of 21 and was the youngest member ever elected to the New York Explorers Club. He is also one of the world's foremost experts on the Himalayas, where he has led 14 major expeditions. Peissel has written 14 books, which have been published in 83 editions in 15 countries.

When not found in their fisherman's house in Cadaqués, Spain, with their two young children, Peissel and Allen can be found trekking across the Himalayas or traveling in Central America.

ACKNOWLEDGMENTS
The authors would like to thank Lisa Bateman for her editorial assistance; Brian Rankin for his careful typing; and Linnie Greason, Heather Moulton, and Luis Abiega for so kindly allowing their lives to be infiltrated by these creepy crawlies and ferocious fauna.

CREDITS
All the original watercolor illustrations are by Michel Peissel. The geo–graphic distribution maps are by Diana Blume.